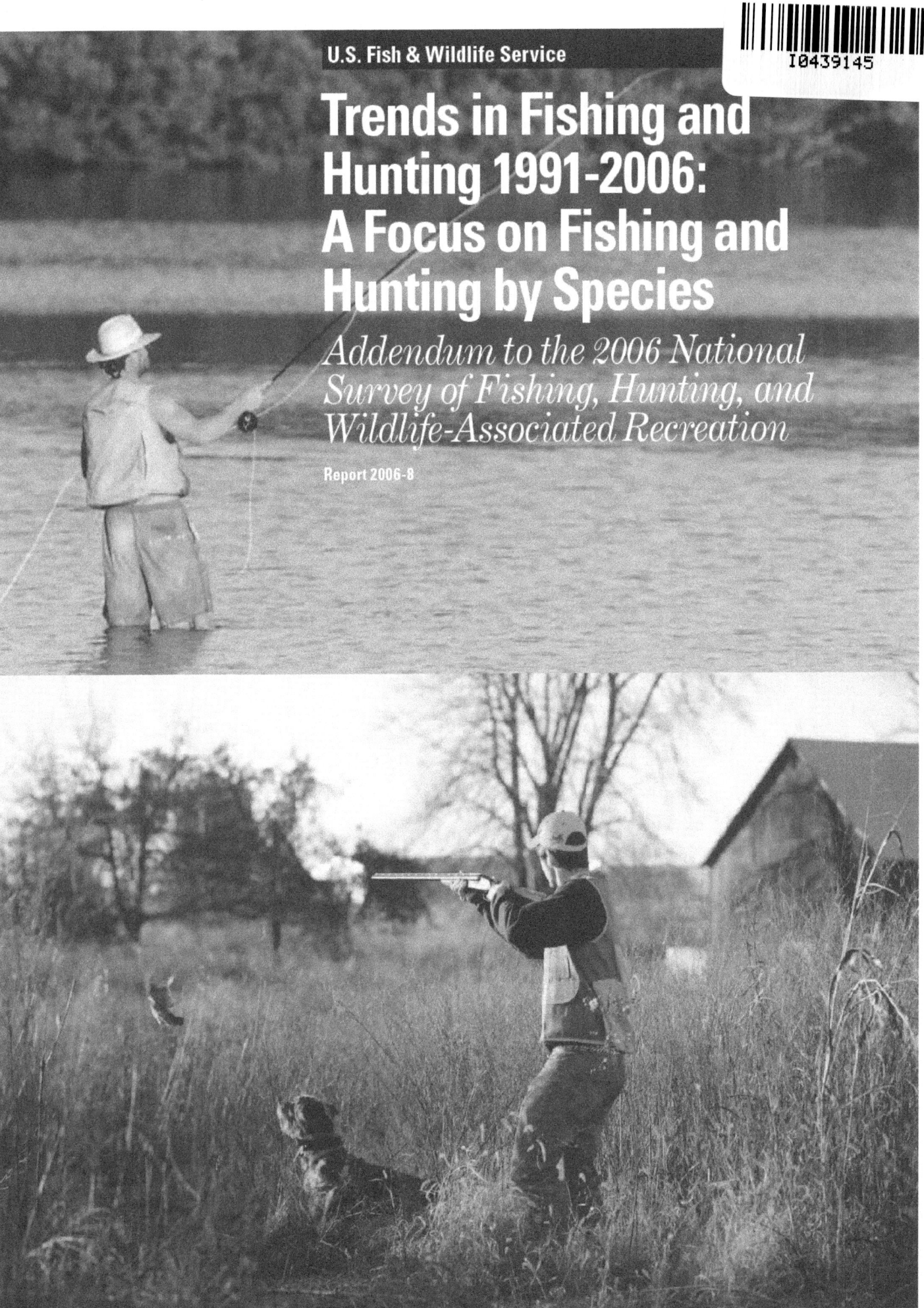

U.S. Fish & Wildlife Service

Trends in Fishing and Hunting 1991-2006: A Focus on Fishing and Hunting by Species

Addendum to the 2006 National Survey of Fishing, Hunting, and Wildlife-Associated Recreation

Report 2006-8

Trends in Fishing and Hunting 1991-2006: A Focus on Fishing and Hunting by Species

Addendum to the 2006 National Survey of Fishing, Hunting, and Wildlife-Associated Recreation

Report 2006-8

December 2010

Richard Aiken
703-358-1839

This report is intended to complement the National and State Reports for the 2006 National Survey of Fishing, Hunting and Wildlife-Associated Recreation. The conclusions are the author's and do not represent official positions of the U.S. Fish and Wildlife Service.

The author wishes to thank Sylvia Cabrera and Anna Harris for providing helpful advise on different aspects of this report.

Contents

Trends in Fishing and Hunting 1991–2006:
A Focus on Fishing and Hunting by Species **3**

National Hunting and Fishing Trends 1991–2006 3

National Hunting and Fishing Trends by Species 1991–2006 4

National and State Trends by Species Sought **5**

Fishing 5

Hunting 13

Fishing days 22

Hunting days 26

Fishing Expenditures 29

Hunting Expenditures 33

State Participation Trends **36**

Hunting Participation Rates 36

Fishing Participation Rates 48

Demographic Trends **60**

Fishing 60

Hunting 63

Crossover Activity of Hunters and Anglers 66

Conclusion **67**

Trends in Fishing and Hunting 1991-2006: A Focus on Fishing and Hunting by Species

The National Survey of Fishing, Hunting, and Wildlife-Associated Recreation dates back to 1955, and has been repeated at five-year intervals since. The first four Surveys collected only national fishing and hunting data. Beginning in 1975 state-level data was acquired, and beginning in 1980 wildlife watching was added.

This report is concerned only with fishing and hunting trends. Figure 1 shows the trends of the general population, anglers, and hunters since 1955, indexed with 1955=100.

Fishing participation increased faster than the general population, and hunting kept pace with the general population, until 1991. Since 1991 both have had a downward trend. This report looks closer at data from the 1991–2006 Surveys, to get a clearer picture of why this downturn is happening.

National Hunting and Fishing Trends 1991–2006

Fishing and hunting both have experienced declines since 1991.

From the perspective of a percentage of the total population, the decline in hunting and fishing is more pronounced. Table 2 details the drop in participation rates of fishing from 21.0% in 1991 to 13.1% in 2006. Participation rates for hunting fell from 7.4% to 5.5%.

Figure 1. Anglers and Hunters: 1955–2006

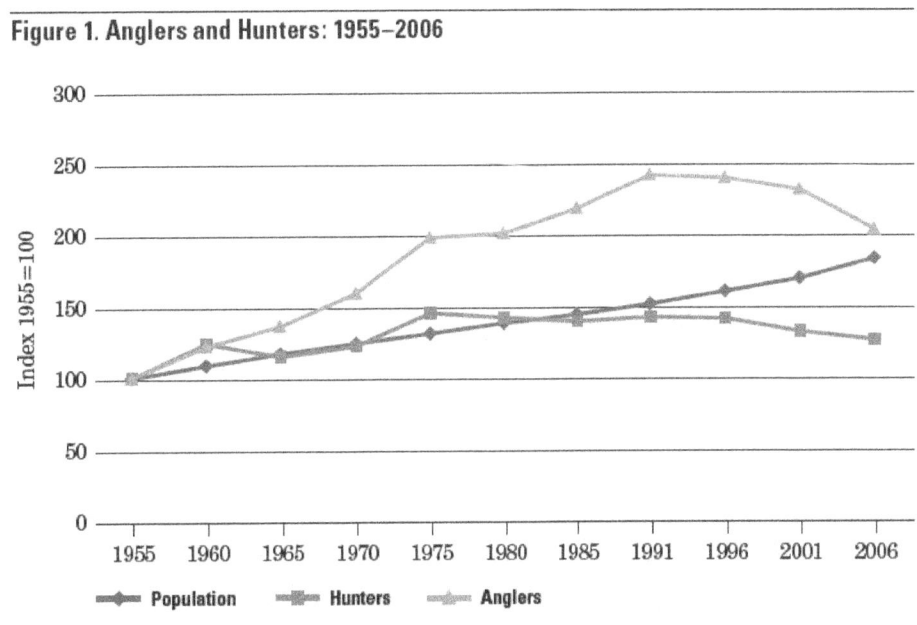

Table 1. Hunters and Anglers 16 years and older: 1991–2006
(numbers in thousands)

Year	Population	Anglers	Hunters
2006	229,245	29,952	12,510
2001	212,298	34,071	13,034
1996	201,472	35,246	13,975
1991	189,966	35,578	14,063

Table 2. Participation Rates 16 years and older: 1991–2006

Year	Anglers	Hunters
2006	13.1%	5.5%
2001	16.0%	6.1%
1996	17.5%	6.9%
1991	21.0%	7.4%

Note: Participation rates are percents of the population that fished or hunted.

National Hunting and Fishing Trends by Species 1991–2006

The National Survey disaggregates hunting into four types: big game, small game, migratory bird, and other animals. Similarly, fishing is categorized as Great Lakes, other freshwater, and saltwater. This report takes the disaggregation further and presents the trend in selected species of game and fish. This will enable us to narrow the focus as we look at the past and future of our hunting and fishing traditions.

The National Survey of Fishing, Hunting, and Wildlife-Associated Recreation tracks hunting and fishing for selected species. For fishing, the list is as follows:

Great Lakes fishing

- black bass
- walleye, sauger
- northern pike, pickerel, muskie, and muskie hybrids
- perch
- salmon
- steelhead
- lake trout
- other trout
- other
- anything

Other freshwater fishing

- black bass
- white bass, striped bass, and striped bass hybrids
- panfish
- crappie
- catfish and bullheads
- walleye
- sauger
- northern pike, pickerel, muskie, and muskie hybrids
- trout
- salmon
- steelhead
- other
- anything

Saltwater fishing

- salmon
- striped bass
- flatfish (flounder, halibut)
- bluefish
- red drum (redfish)
- sea trout (weakfish)
- mackerel
- shellfish
- other
- anything

For hunting:

Big game hunting

- deer
- elk
- bear
- turkey
- other

Small game hunting

- rabbit, hare
- quail
- grouse/prairie chicken
- squirrel
- pheasant
- other

Migratory bird hunting

- geese
- duck
- dove
- other

Other animals, such as fox, raccoon, and groundhog

Some of the most popular species were chosen for this report. "Anything" means the angler was not fishing for any particular species, but for anything that he/she could catch. In this report "freshwater anything anglers" means people who were freshwater fishing for anything. "Saltwater anything anglers" means people who were saltwater fishing for anything. Trend data for all species mentioned above are available. Contact the author for further information.

National and State Trends by Species Sought

While the 1991–2006 trend is the primary area of interest, the 2001–2006 comparison is also presented because it is a measure of the most recent activity trend available.

Fishing

In aggregate, freshwater fishing participation decreased significantly[1] from 1991 to 2006. Looking at the species trends, black bass, trout, catfish, and freshwater anything all had significant decreases both for the 1991–2006 and 2001–2006 comparisons. This consistency, where no species fishing bucked the overall trend, means than no one freshwater fishery was responsible for the downturn and, alternatively, no one fishery has shown a likelihood for an upturn.

_____

[1] Statistical significance in this report is determined at the 95 percent level of significance. For the two survey estimates being compared, 95% of all possible samples would have demonstrated a difference for the two estimates.

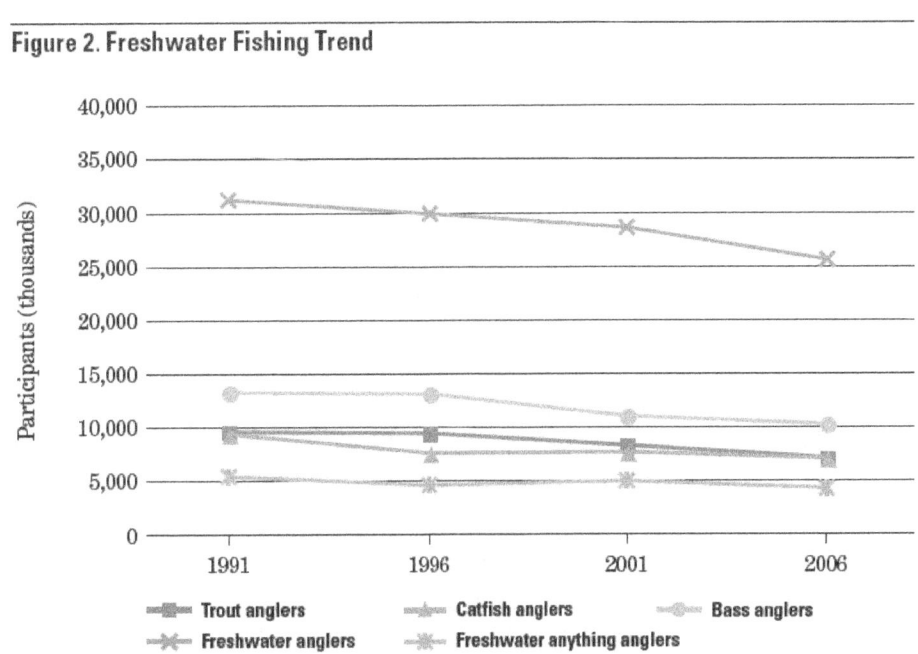

Figure 2. Freshwater Fishing Trend

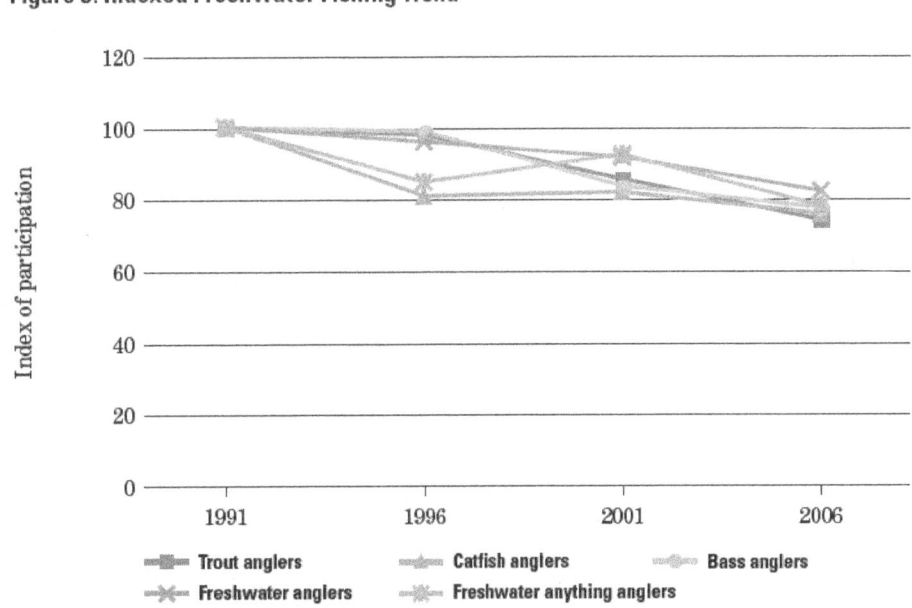

Figure 3. Indexed Freshwater Fishing Trend

Table 3. Trend in the Number of Black Bass Anglers, by State of Activity: 1991–2006
(in 000's)

	1991	1996	2001	2006	2006–1991 Ratio	2006–2001 Ratio
U.S. Total	13,139	12,972	10,956	10,181	0.8	0.9
Alabama	451	455	383	399	0.9	1.0
Alaska	...	...	...	...	N.A.	N.A.
Arizona	180	247	148	152	0.8	1.0
Arkansas	398	335	317	260	0.7	0.8
California	499	653	495	351	0.7	0.7
Colorado	77	84	71	92	1.2	1.3
Connecticut	128	131	112	80	0.6	0.7
Delaware	25	43	28	28	1.1	1.0
Florida	823	663	647	822	1.0	1.3
Georgia	509	496	389	512	1.0	1.3
Hawaii	12	7	...	...	N.A.	N.A.
Idaho	42	73	53	54	1.3	1.0
Illinois	494	620	390	378	0.8	1.0
Indiana	455	507	361	324	0.7	0.9
Iowa	223	218	192	176	0.8	0.9
Kansas	202	188	170	204	1.0	1.2
Kentucky	413	405	339	344	0.8	1.0
Louisiana	408	409	272	187	0.5	0.7
Maine	118	117	107	129	1.1	1.2
Maryland	238	146	155	160	0.7	1.0
Massachusetts	208	228	155	168	0.8	1.1
Michigan	653	568	429	531	0.8	1.2
Minnesota	325	428	345	351	1.1	1.0
Mississippi	263	246	239	214	0.8	0.9
Missouri	650	621	574	376	0.6	0.7
Montana	27	...	22	22	0.8	1.0
Nebraska	96	91	108	66	0.7	0.6
Nevada	48	52	37	30	0.6	0.8
New Hampshire	126	114	97	105	0.8	1.1
New Jersey	185	240	171	138	0.7	0.8
New Mexico	53	73	47	56	1.1	1.2
New York	582	668	507	389	0.7	0.8
North Carolina	548	495	375	348	0.6	0.9
North Dakota	7	6	6	...	N.A.	N.A.
Ohio	632	541	553	457	0.7	0.8
Oklahoma	488	325	381	301	0.6	0.8
Oregon	87	73	63	70	0.8	1.1
Pennsylvania	644	595	559	443	0.7	0.8
Rhode Island	38	49	23	28	0.7	1.2
South Carolina	326	407	285	248	0.8	0.9
South Dakota	26	49	22	17	0.7	0.8
Tennessee	477	399	460	368	0.8	0.8
Texas	1088	1315	892	852	0.8	1.0
Utah	53	46	68	60	1.1	0.9
Vermont	52	66	41	46	0.9	1.1
Virginia	420	446	390	299	0.7	0.8
Washington	122	150	102	75	0.6	0.7
West Virginia	180	151	143	156	0.9	1.1
Wisconsin	495	387	501	420	0.8	0.8
Wyoming	7	...	...	8	1.1	N.A.

N.A. Not available   ... Sample size too small to report data reliably.
The ratios are calculated by dividing the later year's estimate by the earlier year's estimate. The ratio is useful in comparing trends across states.

Table 4. Trend in the Number of Trout Anglers, by State of Activity: 1991–2006

(in 000's)

	1991	1996	2001	2006	2006–1991 Ratio	2006–2001 Ratio
U.S. Total	9,497	9,290	8,118	7,022	0.7	0.9
Alabama	30	30	19	…	N.A.	N.A.
Alaska	108	111	83	66	0.6	0.8
Arizona	228	218	219	209	0.9	1.0
Arkansas	108	152	131	143	1.3	1.1
California	1628	1526	1174	871	0.5	0.7
Colorado	706	699	806	608	0.9	0.8
Connecticut	175	168	118	130	0.7	1.1
Delaware	12	9	11	14	1.2	1.3
Florida	46	…	90	70	1.5	0.8
Georgia	108	160	108	140	1.3	1.3
Hawaii	8	7	…	…	N.A.	N.A.
Idaho	319	409	332	258	0.8	0.8
Illinois	118	178	90	38	0.3	0.4
Indiana	48	43	34	26	0.5	0.8
Iowa	26	48	48	34	1.3	0.7
Kansas	16	…	18	18	1.1	1.0
Kentucky	39	39	41	38	1.0	0.9
Louisiana	48	39	37	72	1.5	1.9
Maine	275	185	163	179	0.7	1.1
Maryland	87	89	101	77	0.9	0.8
Massachusetts	201	179	133	156	0.8	1.2
Michigan	305	288	239	249	0.8	1.0
Minnesota	89	88	78	49	0.6	0.6
Mississippi	14	…	23	…	N.A.	N.A.
Missouri	236	255	195	156	0.7	0.8
Montana	285	266	293	236	0.8	0.8
Nebraska	33	27	25	22	0.7	0.9
Nevada	89	159	111	106	1.2	1.0
New Hampshire	171	131	121	89	0.5	0.7
New Jersey	213	195	140	77	0.4	0.6
New Mexico	213	237	210	184	0.9	0.9
New York	748	560	436	454	0.6	1.0
North Carolina	183	197	173	257	1.4	1.5
North Dakota	4	6	6	…	N.A.	N.A.
Ohio	132	74	101	74	0.6	0.7
Oklahoma	39	…	59	…	N.A.	N.A.
Oregon	428	395	417	320	0.7	0.8
Pennsylvania	879	750	653	613	0.7	0.9
Rhode Island	38	39	22	14	0.4	0.6
South Carolina	46	38	49	21	0.5	0.4
South Dakota	30	42	16	18	0.6	1.1
Tennessee	148	120	137	95	0.6	0.7
Texas	97	141	140	160	1.6	1.1
Utah	263	341	431	328	1.2	0.8
Vermont	116	107	100	60	0.5	0.6
Virginia	177	239	116	138	0.8	1.2
Washington	533	628	436	337	0.6	0.8
West Virginia	143	174	112	177	1.2	1.6
Wisconsin	220	139	200	192	0.9	1.0
Wyoming	268	357	256	179	0.7	0.7

N.A. Not available … Sample size too small to report data reliably.
The ratios are calculated by dividing the later year's estimate by the earlier year's estimate. The ratio is useful in comparing trends across states.

Table 5. Trend in the Number of Catfish Anglers, by State of Activity: 1991–2006
(in 000's)

	1991	1996	2001	2006	2006–1991 Ratio	2006–2001 Ratio
U.S. Total	9,195	7,430	7,517	6,954	0.8	0.9
Alabama	334	331	230	245	0.7	1.1
Alaska	...	...	...	...	N.A.	N.A.
Arizona	221	128	105	119	0.5	1.1
Arkansas	295	274	340	235	0.8	0.7
California	502	441	403	180	0.4	0.4
Colorado	37	48	68	35	0.9	0.5
Connecticut	37	36	13	...	N.A.	N.A.
Delaware	12	9	6	13	1.1	2.2
Florida	304	223	299	389	1.3	1.3
Georgia	352	248	467	395	1.1	0.8
Hawaii	6	6	...	6	1.0	N.A.
Idaho	28	40	32	25	0.9	0.8
Illinois	616	430	421	335	0.5	0.8
Indiana	333	303	277	223	0.7	0.8
Iowa	301	242	196	214	0.7	1.1
Kansas	216	166	216	216	1.0	1.0
Kentucky	310	251	305	275	0.9	0.9
Louisiana	338	288	246	207	0.6	0.8
Maine	10	...	...	...	N.A.	N.A.
Maryland	131	77	64	74	0.6	1.2
Massachusetts	51	24	27	27	0.5	1.0
Michigan	134	...	...	64	0.5	N.A.
Minnesota	60	33	38	71	1.2	1.9
Mississippi	276	194	277	215	0.8	0.8
Missouri	540	411	467	448	0.8	1.0
Montana	6	...	12	...	N.A.	N.A.
Nebraska	135	80	107	69	0.5	0.6
Nevada	23	23	28	23	1.0	0.8
New Hampshire	24	11	...	...	N.A.	N.A.
New Jersey	73	48	35	44	0.6	1.3
New Mexico	48	72	60	59	1.2	1.0
New York	183	128	82	72	0.4	0.9
North Carolina	308	269	275	294	1.0	1.1
North Dakota	7	9	8	...	N.A.	N.A.
Ohio	416	248	342	288	0.7	0.8
Oklahoma	418	510	321	264	0.6	0.8
Oregon	43	...	35	30	0.7	0.9
Pennsylvania	255	156	165	143	0.6	0.9
Rhode Island	4	4	...	...	N.A.	N.A.
South Carolina	238	210	273	226	0.9	0.8
South Dakota	37	32	25	19	0.5	0.8
Tennessee	387	223	261	298	0.8	1.1
Texas	1149	1136	974	1035	0.9	1.1
Utah	44	32	48	54	1.2	1.1
Vermont	18	7	10	...	N.A.	N.A.
Virginia	225	181	185	153	0.7	0.8
Washington	42	...	...	23	0.5	N.A.
West Virginia	116	87	89	108	0.9	1.2
Wisconsin	137	82	54	46	0.3	0.9
Wyoming	13	...	...	...	N.A.	N.A.

N.A. Not available   ... Sample size too small to report data reliably.
The ratios are calculated by dividing the later year's estimate by the earlier year's estimate. The ratio is useful in comparing trends across states.

Table 6. Trend in Number of Freshwater Anything Anglers, by State of Activity: 1991–2006
(in 000's)

	1991	1996	2001	2006	2006–1991 Ratio	2006–2001 Ratio
U.S. Total	**5,285**	**4,475**	**4,872**	**4,120**	**0.8**	**0.8**
Alabama	107	128	141	115	1.1	0.8
Alaska	26	19	12	...	N.A.	N.A.
Arizona	65	70	85	59	0.9	0.7
Arkansas	109	68	123	117	1.1	1.0
California	144	220	192	87	0.6	0.5
Colorado	50	56	113	23	0.5	0.2
Connecticut	24	85	55	32	1.3	0.6
Delaware	7	16	24	14	2.0	0.6
Florida	300	203	480	268	0.9	0.6
Georgia	255	175	209	202	0.8	1.0
Hawaii	9	...	5	...	N.A.	N.A.
Idaho	17	...	...	30	1.8	N.A.
Illinois	283	231	262	138	0.5	0.5
Indiana	186	120	101	106	0.6	1.0
Iowa	116	55	96	52	0.4	0.5
Kansas	66	36	57	45	0.7	0.8
Kentucky	140	198	124	116	0.8	0.9
Louisiana	100	137	89	67	0.7	0.8
Maine	40	50	40	46	1.2	1.2
Maryland	64	62	99	70	1.1	0.7
Massachusetts	67	79	80	52	0.8	0.7
Michigan	243	225	181	209	0.9	1.2
Minnesota	147	153	90	149	1.0	1.7
Mississippi	114	70	99	74	0.6	0.7
Missouri	224	101	127	160	0.7	1.3
Montana	28	36	55	13	0.5	0.2
Nebraska	40	21	65	52	1.3	0.8
Nevada	...	...	...	11	N.A.	N.A.
New Hampshire	34	43	48	25	0.7	0.5
New Jersey	77	58	81	44	0.6	0.5
New Mexico	16	24	25	14	0.9	0.6
New York	312	257	171	132	0.4	0.8
North Carolina	200	153	154	167	0.8	1.1
North Dakota	15	6	23	9	0.6	0.4
Ohio	379	165	206	290	0.8	1.4
Oklahoma	118	142	254	118	1.0	0.5
Oregon	21	...	44	43	2.0	1.0
Pennsylvania	257	280	231	67	0.3	0.3
Rhode Island	9	7	15	11	1.2	0.7
South Carolina	78	111	129	122	1.6	0.9
South Dakota	28	9	20	17	0.6	0.9
Tennessee	201	98	120	227	1.1	1.9
Texas	318	322	258	285	0.9	1.1
Utah	18	22	28	21	1.2	0.8
Vermont	27	23	40	17	0.6	0.4
Virginia	172	157	128	163	0.9	1.3
Washington	59	...	42	29	0.5	0.7
West Virginia	56	46	60	72	1.3	1.2
Wisconsin	213	180	129	166	0.8	1.3
Wyoming	25	11	...	17	0.7	N.A.

N.A. Not available   ... Sample size too small to report data reliably.
The ratios are calculated by dividing the later year's estimate by the earlier year's estimate. The ratio is useful in comparing trends across states.

In aggregate, saltwater fishing participation also significantly decreased from 1991 to 2006. At the species level there was a difference. Flatfishing participation did not decrease significantly either from 1991 to 2006 or 2001 to 2006. Fishing for saltwater anything decreased significantly. Looking at all saltwater species fishing, bluefish and mackerel fishing has gone way down, contributing significantly to the overall downward trend.

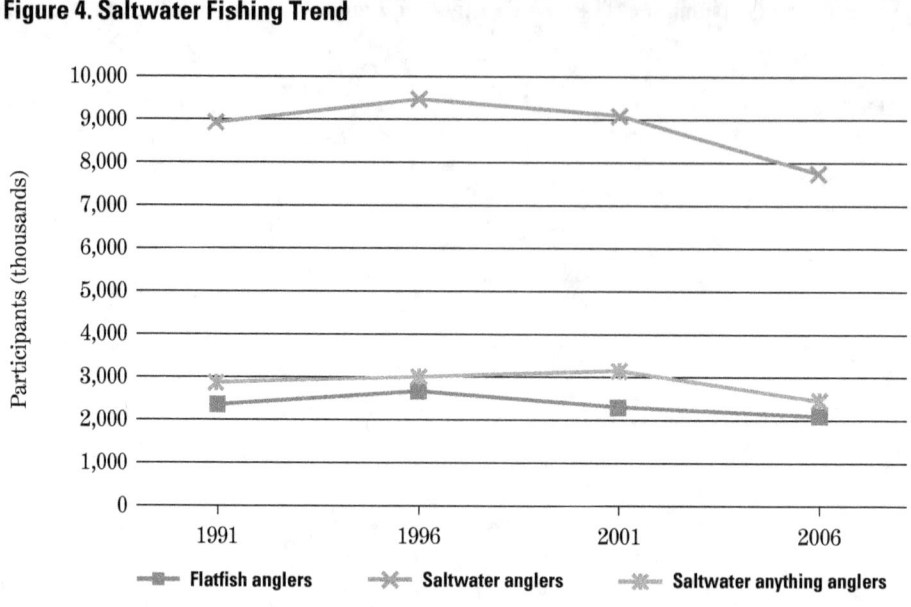

Figure 4. Saltwater Fishing Trend

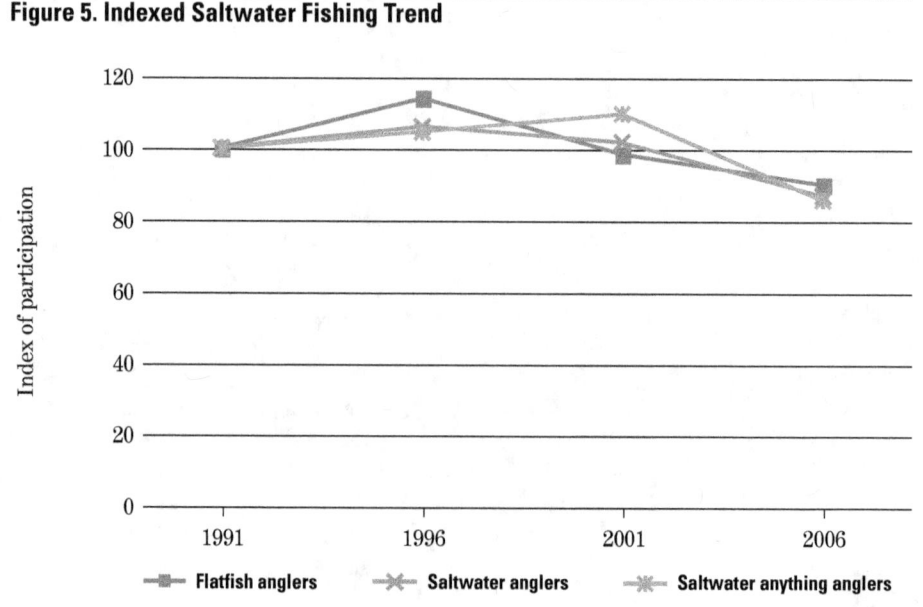

Figure 5. Indexed Saltwater Fishing Trend

Table 7. Trend in Number of Saltwater Anything Anglers, by State of Activity: 1991–2006
(in 000's)

	1991	1996	2001	2006	2006–1991 Ratio	2006–2001 Ratio
U.S. Total	**2,831**	**2,964**	**3,110**	**2,424**	**0.9**	**0.8**
Alabama	69	81	89	61	0.9	0.7
Alaska	25	6	...	...	N.A.	N.A.
California	343	346	314	245	0.7	0.8
Connecticut	17	39	47	22	1.3	0.5
Delaware	39	18	30	45	1.2	1.5
Florida	973	1086	1278	920	0.9	0.7
Georgia	27	51	35	71	2.6	2.0
Hawaii	110	92	68	53	0.5	0.8
Louisiana	74	93	143	65	0.9	0.5
Maine	28	...	15	20	0.7	1.3
Maryland	98	96	134	102	1.0	0.8
Massachusetts	65	75	59	57	0.9	1.0
Mississippi	53	39	45	35	0.7	0.8
New Hampshire	...	...	...	13	N.A.	N.A.
New Jersey	86	123	150	99	1.2	0.7
New York	...	77	72	46	N.A.	0.6
North Carolina	224	286	260	187	0.8	0.7
Oregon	22	...	25	...	N.A.	N.A.
Rhode Island	23	8	25	24	1.0	1.0
South Carolina	110	132	146	134	1.2	0.9
Texas	308	261	148	204	0.7	1.4
Virginia	110	107	117	140	1.3	1.2
Washington	53	49	28	...	N.A.	N.A.

N.A. Not available   ... Sample size too small to report data reliably.
The ratios are calculated by dividing the later year's estimate by the earlier year's estimate. The ratio is useful in comparing trends across states.

Table 8. Trend in Number of Flatfish Anglers, by State of Activity: 1991–2006
(in 000's)

	1991	1996	2001	2006	2006–1991 Ratio	2006–2001 Ratio
U.S. Total	2,302	2,626	2,269	2,069	0.9	0.9
Alabama	33	27	29	47	1.4	1.6
Alaska	109	143	159	113	1.0	0.7
California	176	214	191	202	1.1	1.1
Connecticut	38	51	42	35	0.9	0.8
Delaware	49	77	56	67	1.4	1.2
Florida	266	307	322	232	0.9	0.7
Georgia	...	...	...	...	N.A.	N.A.
Hawaii	...	...	...	...	N.A.	N.A.
Louisiana	71	56	62	61	0.9	1.0
Maine	...	10	...	...	N.A.	N.A.
Maryland	95	132	84	97	1.0	1.2
Massachusetts	81	74	71	68	0.8	1.0
Mississippi	35	40	18	...	N.A.	N.A.
New Hampshire	18	...	...	...	N.A.	N.A.
New Jersey	382	444	285	288	0.8	1.0
New York	214	209	206	110	0.5	0.5
North Carolina	208	291	190	140	0.7	0.7
Oregon	14	...	...	...	N.A.	N.A.
Rhode Island	34	20	39	34	1.0	0.9
South Carolina	73	95	90	59	0.8	0.7
Texas	333	385	300	463	1.4	1.5
Virginia	92	143	152	94	1.0	0.6
Washington	60	...	26	...	N.A.	N.A.

Note: the 1991–2006 and 2001–2006 U.S. totals are not statistically significantly different.
N.A. Not available   ... Sample size too small to report data reliably.
The ratios are calculated by dividing the later year's estimate by the earlier year's estimate. The ratio is useful in comparing trends across states.

Hunting

Big game hunting as a single category had no significant differences in participation from 1991 to 2006 or 2001 to 2006. The same is true with deer hunting. Turkey hunting underwent a significant increase 1991–2006 and had no significant difference 2001–2006. Deer hunting (the major component of big game hunting) had the same stable trend as overall big game hunting.

Figure 6. Big Game Hunting Trend

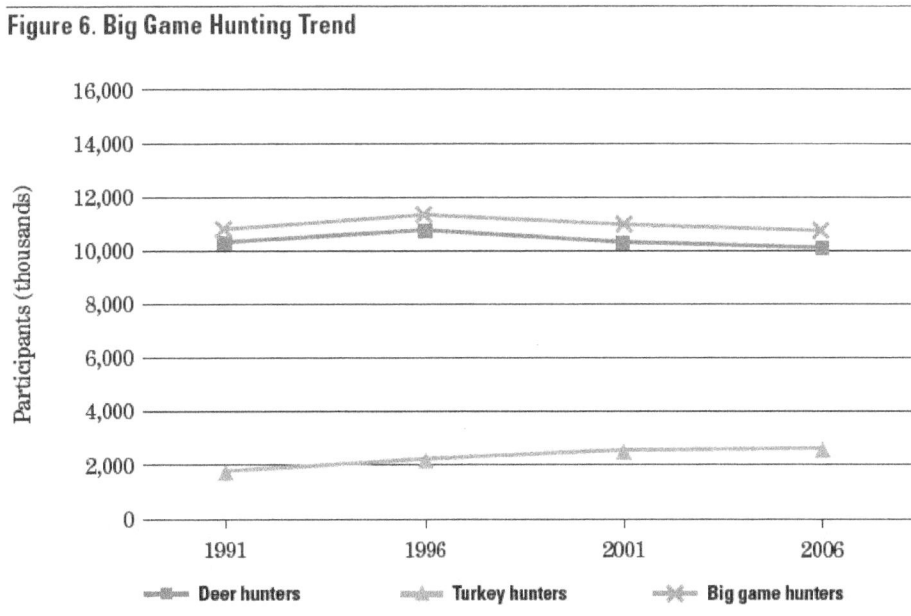

Figure 7. Indexed Big Game Hunting Trend

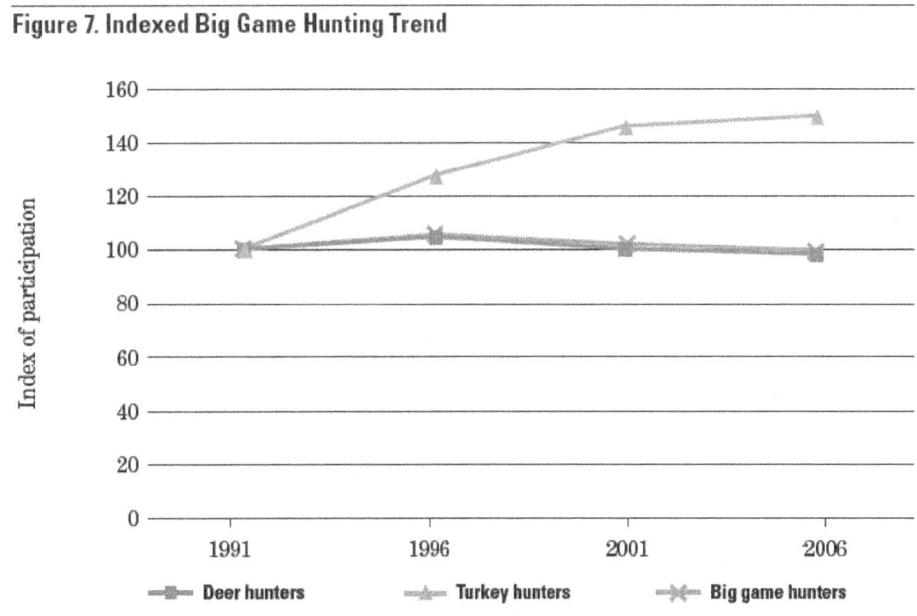

Table 9. Trend in Number of Deer Hunters, by State of Activity: 1991–2006
(in 000's)

	1991	1996	2001	2006	2006–1991 Ratio	2006–2001 Ratio
U.S. Total	**10,277**	**10,722**	**10,272**	**10,062**	**1.0**	**1.0**
Alabama	249	269	379	334	1.3	0.9
Alaska	9	15	19	17	1.9	0.9
Arizona	90	74	63	76	0.8	1.2
Arkansas	243	296	314	277	1.1	0.9
California	186	239	85	107	0.6	1.3
Colorado	208	243	99	66	0.3	0.7
Connecticut	30	42	27	21	0.7	0.8
Delaware	16	28	11	24	1.5	2.2
Florida	180	130	156	168	0.9	1.1
Georgia	323	322	332	405	1.3	1.2
Hawaii	5	11	7	9	1.8	1.3
Idaho	149	183	125	119	0.8	1.0
Illinois	248	256	238	204	0.8	0.9
Indiana	204	262	215	231	1.1	1.1
Iowa	149	187	133	165	1.1	1.2
Kansas	63	100	140	118	1.9	0.8
Kentucky	205	271	231	238	1.2	1.0
Louisiana	199	228	207	202	1.0	1.0
Maine	154	169	145	160	1.0	1.1
Maryland	97	109	126	125	1.3	1.0
Massachusetts	82	76	56	57	0.7	1.0
Michigan	742	839	667	713	1.0	1.1
Minnesota	335	473	475	415	1.2	0.9
Mississippi	295	345	288	276	0.9	1.0
Missouri	364	416	373	492	1.4	1.3
Montana	178	135	154	162	0.9	1.1
Nebraska	63	74	78	63	1.0	0.8
Nevada	27	28	25	26	1.0	1.0
New Hampshire	60	65	67	52	0.9	0.8
New Jersey	101	75	111	67	0.7	0.6
New Mexico	62	56	75	31	0.5	0.4
New York	651	576	651	506	0.8	0.8
North Carolina	280	259	207	215	0.8	1.0
North Dakota	57	58	74	74	1.3	1.0
Ohio	386	312	417	426	1.1	1.0
Oklahoma	125	224	199	181	1.4	0.9
Oregon	195	221	183	164	0.8	0.9
Pennsylvania	937	810	932	978	1.0	1.0
Rhode Island	15	20	6	11	0.7	1.8
South Carolina	177	228	207	161	0.9	0.8
South Dakota	66	68	68	57	0.9	0.8
Tennessee	220	266	228	242	1.1	1.1
Texas	722	752	860	814	1.1	0.9
Utah	147	109	139	102	0.7	0.7
Vermont	90	89	92	63	0.7	0.7
Virginia	309	326	313	345	1.1	1.1
Washington	177	214	156	150	0.8	1.0
West Virginia	294	343	259	244	0.8	0.9
Wisconsin	665	552	596	620	0.9	1.0
Wyoming	88	62	66	55	0.6	0.8

N.A. Not available ... Sample size too small to report data reliably.
The ratios are calculated by dividing the later year's estimate by the earlier year's estimate. The ratio is useful in comparing trends across states.

Table 10. Trend in Number of Turkey Hunters, by State of Activity: 1991–2006
(in 000's)

	1991	1996	2001	2006	2006–1991 Ratio	2006–2001 Ratio
U.S. Total	1,720	2,189	2,504	2,569	1.5	1.0
Alabama	64	59	80	98	1.5	1.2
Alaska	...	...	...	...	N.A.	N.A.
Arizona	9	...	...	...	N.A.	N.A.
Arkansas	37	76	106	86	2.3	0.8
California	...	...	...	51	N.A.	N.A.
Colorado	...	...	...	...	N.A.	N.A.
Connecticut	...	10	...	...	N.A.	N.A.
Delaware	...	...	...	...	N.A.	N.A.
Florida	39	...	96	82	2.1	0.9
Georgia	49	61	83	79	1.6	1.0
Hawaii	...	...	...	...	N.A.	N.A.
Idaho	...	...	13	25	N.A.	1.9
Illinois	23	...	...	61	2.7	N.A.
Indiana	19	...	37	35	1.8	0.9
Iowa	22	51	25	51	2.3	2.0
Kansas	18	31	58	51	2.8	0.9
Kentucky	17	73	105	76	4.5	0.7
Louisiana	12	...	31	47	3.9	1.5
Maine	...	...	...	21	N.A.	N.A.
Maryland	23	29	20	25	1.1	1.3
Massachusetts	15	...	...	14	0.9	N.A.
Michigan	36	...	68	81	2.3	1.2
Minnesota	...	...	...	...	N.A.	N.A.
Mississippi	63	89	95	67	1.1	0.7
Missouri	137	169	165	155	1.1	0.9
Montana	5	...	...	...	N.A.	N.A.
Nebraska	14	8	16	22	1.6	1.4
Nevada	...	...	...	...	N.A.	N.A.
New Hampshire	...	...	12	13	N.A.	1.1
New Jersey	...	...	...	27	N.A.	N.A.
New Mexico	11	...	13	23	2.1	1.8
New York	141	215	270	164	1.2	0.6
North Carolina	30	...	53	75	2.5	1.4
North Dakota	...	...	...	7	N.A.	N.A.
Ohio	25	77	92	96	3.8	1.0
Oklahoma	28	57	76	72	2.6	0.9
Oregon	...	...	17	...	N.A.	N.A.
Pennsylvania	346	343	301	369	1.1	1.2
Rhode Island	...	...	...	...	N.A.	N.A.
South Carolina	36	53	46	64	1.8	1.4
South Dakota	7	13	10	12	1.7	1.2
Tennessee	34	43	86	120	3.5	1.4
Texas	179	108	128	182	1.0	1.4
Utah	...	...	...	...	N.A.	N.A.
Vermont	11	8	16	15	1.4	0.9
Virginia	160	151	103	120	0.8	1.2
Washington	...	...	18	...	N.A.	N.A.
West Virginia	98	117	79	73	0.7	0.9
Wisconsin	49	93	119	159	3.2	1.3
Wyoming	4	...	6	...	N.A.	N.A.

N.A. Not available   ... Sample size too small to report data reliably.
The ratios are calculated by dividing the later year's estimate by the earlier year's estimate. The ratio is useful in comparing trends across states.

Small game hunting in aggregate had significant decreases for both 1991–2006 and 2001–2006. Rabbit and squirrel hunting had significant decreases in participation for 1991–2006. In the more recent interval of 2001–2006, squirrel hunting had significant decreases but rabbit hunting did not. Squirrel hunting and, to a lesser extent, rabbit hunting have been the root cause of the downward trend in small game hunting.

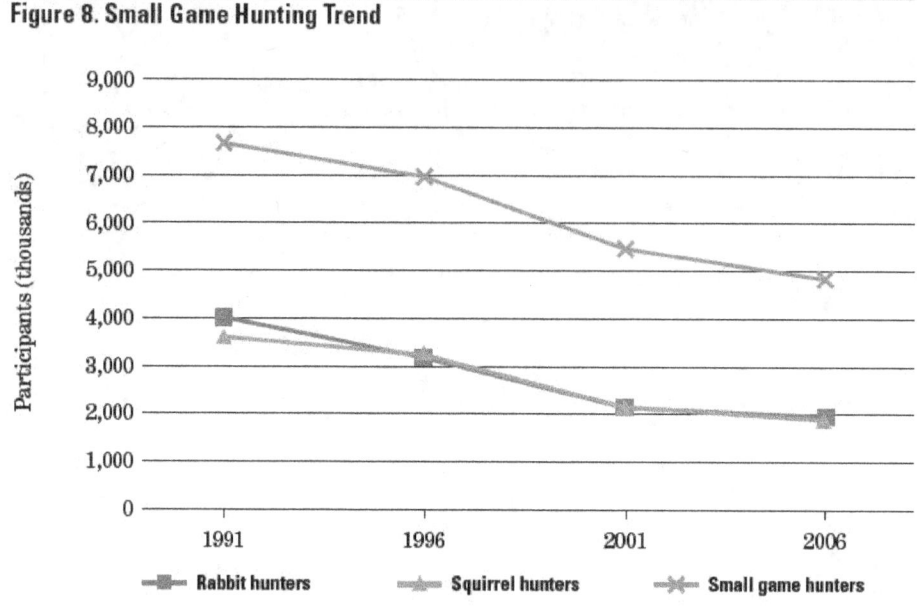

Figure 8. Small Game Hunting Trend

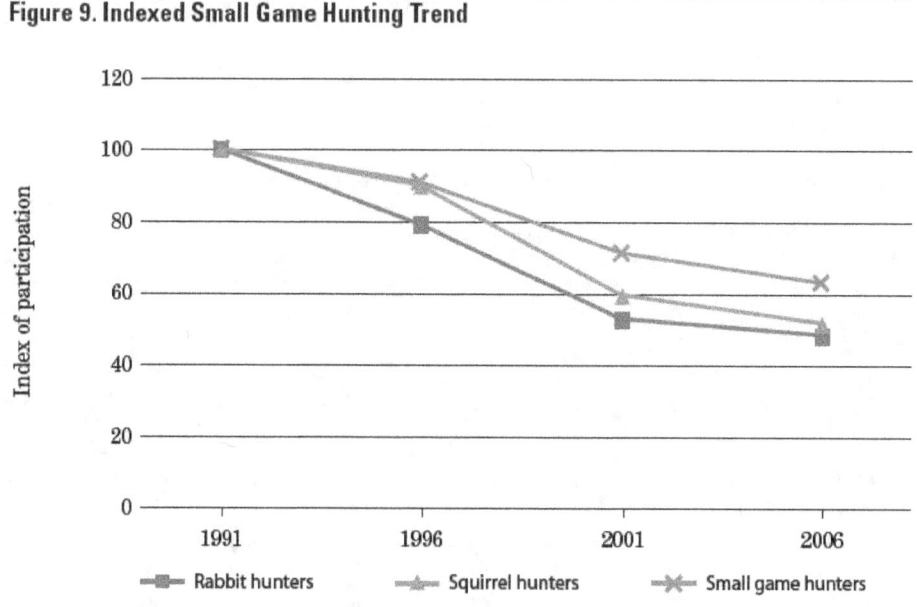

Figure 9. Indexed Small Game Hunting Trend

Table 11. Trend in Number of Rabbit Hunters, by State of Activity: 1991–2006
(in 000's)

	1991	1996	2001	2006	2006–1991 Ratio	2006–2001 Ratio
U.S. Total	**3,980**	**3,146**	**2,099**	**1,923**	**0.5**	**0.9**
Alabama	90	27	47	66	0.7	1.4
Alaska	10	11	7	...	N.A.	N.A.
Arizona	25	23	21	18	0.7	0.9
Arkansas	55	80	49	28	0.5	0.6
California	64	...	...	...	N.A.	N.A.
Colorado	34	47	23	...	N.A.	N.A.
Connecticut	...	...	...	...	N.A.	N.A.
Delaware	8	11	3	5	0.6	1.7
Florida	37	...	...	...	N.A.	N.A.
Georgia	70	...	55	65	0.9	1.2
Hawaii	...	...	...	...	N.A.	N.A.
Idaho	18	21	...	...	N.A.	N.A.
Illinois	159	166	...	55	0.3	N.A.
Indiana	157	123	100	53	0.3	0.5
Iowa	109	114	49	32	0.3	0.7
Kansas	60	56	34	29	0.5	0.9
Kentucky	150	138	97	63	0.4	0.6
Louisiana	138	149	68	86	0.6	1.3
Maine	24	20	17	12	0.5	0.7
Maryland	35	21	26	17	0.5	0.7
Massachusetts	26	...	...	...	N.A.	N.A.
Michigan	321	318	130	131	0.4	1.0
Minnesota	37	...	...	...	N.A.	N.A.
Mississippi	118	132	110	49	0.4	0.4
Missouri	158	175	96	101	0.6	1.1
Montana	13	...	...	...	N.A.	N.A.
Nebraska	31	20	10	11	0.4	1.1
Nevada	12	...	...	7	0.6	N.A.
New Hampshire	14	16	...	...	N.A.	N.A.
New Jersey	54	32	27	...	N.A.	N.A.
New Mexico	19	8	...	12	0.6	N.A.
New York	216	173	160	107	0.5	0.7
North Carolina	107	117	58	52	0.5	0.9
North Dakota	6	...	5	...	N.A.	N.A.
Ohio	373	235	208	127	0.3	0.6
Oklahoma	64	65	51	29	0.5	0.6
Oregon	10	...	...	...	N.A.	N.A.
Pennsylvania	473	241	224	235	0.5	1.0
Rhode Island	5	3	...	...	N.A.	N.A.
South Carolina	40	40	41	30	0.8	0.7
South Dakota	14	13	...	...	N.A.	N.A.
Tennessee	124	118	67	66	0.5	1.0
Texas	148	...	...	122	0.8	N.A.
Utah	42	33	27	37	0.9	1.4
Vermont	26	19	14	...	N.A.	N.A.
Virginia	108	57	41	70	0.6	1.7
Washington	16	...	...	...	N.A.	N.A.
West Virginia	87	45	50	43	0.5	0.9
Wisconsin	155	163	64	67	0.4	1.0
Wyoming	13	8	13	7	0.5	0.5

Note: the 2001–2006 U.S. total difference is not statistically significant.
N.A. Not available   ... Sample size too small to report data reliably.
The ratios are calculated by dividing the later year's estimate by the earlier year's estimate. The ratio is useful in comparing trends across states.

Table 12. Trend in Number of Squirrel Hunters, by State of Activity: 1991–2006
(in 000's)

	1991	1996	2001	2006	2006–1991 Ratio	2006–2001 Ratio
U.S. Total	3,569	3,207	2,119	1,845	0.5	0.9
Alabama	96	56	60	86	0.9	1.4
Alaska	...	...	...	...	N.A.	N.A.
Arizona	...	...	...	...	N.A.	N.A.
Arkansas	117	143	125	92	0.8	0.7
California	62	...	...	...	N.A.	N.A.
Colorado	...	...	...	...	N.A.	N.A.
Connecticut	8	...	...	...	N.A.	N.A.
Delaware	7	13	...	...	N.A.	N.A.
Florida	85	...	...	49	0.6	N.A.
Georgia	82	86	80	86	1.0	1.1
Hawaii	...	...	...	...	N.A.	N.A.
Idaho	13	...	...	...	N.A.	N.A.
Illinois	136	163	...	44	0.3	N.A.
Indiana	140	122	94	55	0.4	0.6
Iowa	76	77	33	23	0.3	0.7
Kansas	31	26	23	...	N.A.	N.A.
Kentucky	167	146	92	72	0.4	0.8
Louisiana	167	191	88	90	0.5	1.0
Maine	...	...	...	...	N.A.	N.A.
Maryland	46	29	19	28	0.6	1.5
Massachusetts	12	...	...	...	N.A.	N.A.
Michigan	189	224	92	91	0.5	1.0
Minnesota	52	44	...	...	N.A.	N.A.
Mississippi	156	146	111	65	0.4	0.6
Missouri	168	193	110	152	0.9	1.4
Montana	...	...	...	...	N.A.	N.A.
Nebraska	16	...	...	...	N.A.	N.A.
Nevada	...	...	...	...	N.A.	N.A.
New Hampshire	8	...	...	...	N.A.	N.A.
New Jersey	19	...	...	...	N.A.	N.A.
New Mexico	...	...	...	...	N.A.	N.A.
New York	121	129	101	...	N.A.	N.A.
North Carolina	152	166	73	42	0.3	0.6
North Dakota	...	...	...	...	N.A.	N.A.
Ohio	209	177	171	115	0.6	0.7
Oklahoma	62	73	51	29	0.5	0.6
Oregon	10	...	...	...	N.A.	N.A.
Pennsylvania	365	258	215	203	0.6	0.9
Rhode Island	3	...	...	...	N.A.	N.A.
South Carolina	49	56	52	23	0.5	0.4
South Dakota	4	...	...	...	N.A.	N.A.
Tennessee	163	135	112	78	0.5	0.7
Texas	156	...	...	66	0.4	N.A.
Utah	...	...	...	...	N.A.	N.A.
Vermont	8	11	12	...	N.A.	N.A.
Virginia	156	110	88	78	0.5	0.9
Washington	...	...	...	...	N.A.	N.A.
West Virginia	162	181	109	114	0.7	1.0
Wisconsin	138	145	62	60	0.4	1.0
Wyoming	...	...	...	...	N.A.	N.A.

N.A. Not available   ... Sample size too small to report data reliably.
The ratios are calculated by dividing the later year's estimate by the earlier year's estimate. The ratio is useful in comparing trends across states.

As with small game hunting, migratory bird hunting had significant decreases from 1991 to 2006. Duck hunting had no significant difference from 1991 to 2006, although in the most recent time interval, 2001–2006, there was a significant decrease. Conversely, dove hunting had a significant decrease in participation for 1991 to 2006, although no significant difference for 2001 to 2006. Dove and duck hunting combined create the overall downward trend. Dove hunting pulled down migratory bird hunting levels over the longer-term, and duck hunting pulled it down in the most recent time period.

Figure 10. Migratory Bird Hunting Trend

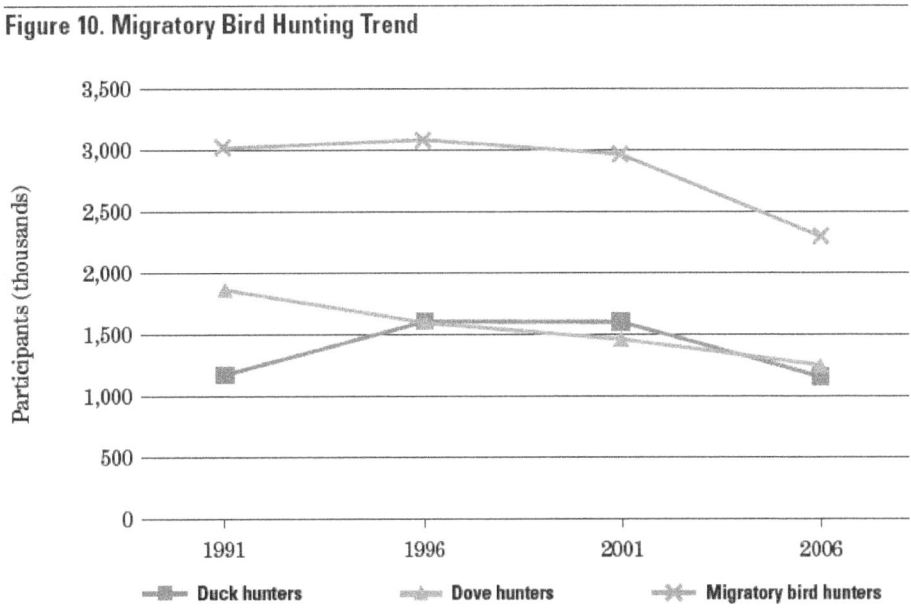

Figure 11. Indexed Migratory Bird Hunting Trend

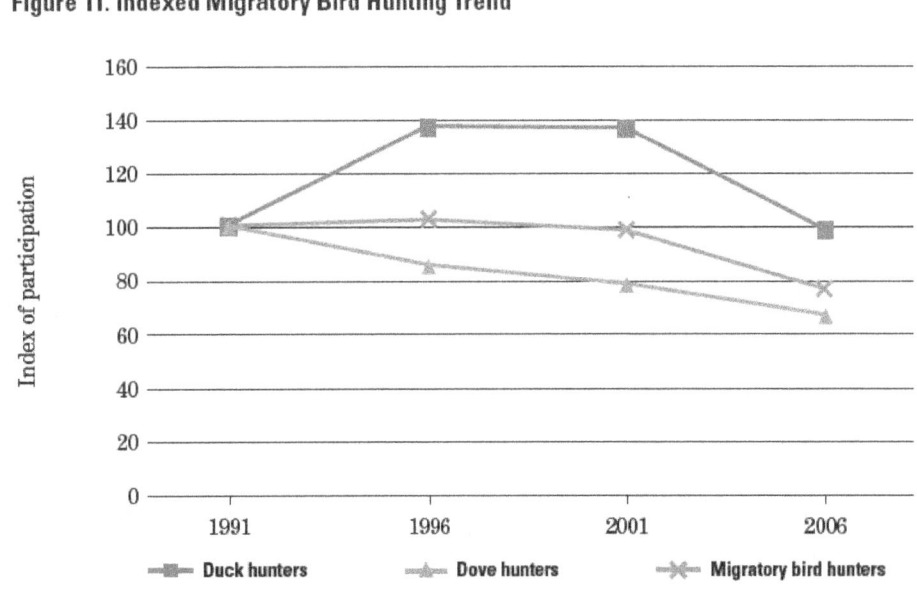

Table 13. Trend in Number of Duck Hunters, by State of Activity: 1991–2006
(in 000's)

	1991	1996	2001	2006	2006–1991 Ratio	2006–2001 Ratio
U.S. Total	**1,164**	**1,596**	**1,589**	**1,147**	**1.0**	**0.7**
Alabama	...	...	27	24	N.A.	0.9
Alaska	12	10	11	...	N.A.	N.A.
Arizona	...	...	...	...	N.A.	N.A.
Arkansas	46	78	154	100	2.2	0.6
California	97	131	97	61	0.6	0.6
Colorado	28	33	33	...	N.A.	N.A.
Connecticut	5	...	...	...	N.A.	N.A.
Delaware	8	13	...	10	1.3	N.A.
Florida	...	...	...	...	N.A.	N.A.
Georgia	20	...	...	...	N.A.	N.A.
Hawaii	...	...	...	...	N.A.	N.A.
Idaho	19	33	28	26	1.4	0.9
Illinois	55	52	39	65	1.2	1.7
Indiana	...	...	...	...	N.A.	N.A.
Iowa	23	31	45	...	N.A.	N.A.
Kansas	10	...	26	27	2.7	1.0
Kentucky	18	20	23	...	N.A.	N.A.
Louisiana	74	111	127	72	1.0	0.6
Maine	10	...	...	...	N.A.	N.A.
Maryland	14	46	33	39	2.8	1.2
Massachusetts	15	...	...	13	0.9	N.A.
Michigan	45	...	...	...	N.A.	N.A.
Minnesota	66	132	165	49	0.7	0.3
Mississippi	35	59	39	41	1.2	1.1
Missouri	26	...	35	36	1.4	1.0
Montana	17	24	16	13	0.8	0.8
Nebraska	22	27	33	28	1.3	0.8
Nevada	8	9	13	...	N.A.	N.A.
New Hampshire	5	5	...	...	N.A.	N.A.
New Jersey	17	...	...	...	N.A.	N.A.
New Mexico	6	...	15	...	N.A.	N.A.
New York	36	...	55	...	N.A.	N.A.
North Carolina	25	...	48	...	N.A.	N.A.
North Dakota	18	17	49	20	1.1	0.4
Ohio	29	...	43	...	N.A.	N.A.
Oklahoma	20	...	32	34	1.7	1.1
Oregon	23	52	29	27	1.2	0.9
Pennsylvania	35	...	...	...	N.A.	N.A.
Rhode Island	2	...	...	...	N.A.	N.A.
South Carolina	25	44	21	32	1.3	1.5
South Dakota	20	30	34	14	0.7	0.4
Tennessee	16	...	54	33	2.1	0.6
Texas	100	101	90	102	1.0	1.1
Utah	9	20	42	20	2.2	0.5
Vermont	4	9	...	...	N.A.	N.A.
Virginia	15	...	...	26	1.7	N.A.
Washington	35	53	42	18	0.5	0.4
West Virginia	...	...	...	...	N.A.	N.A.
Wisconsin	73	79	46	48	0.7	1.0
Wyoming	3	18	...	...	N.A.	N.A.

N.A. Not available   ... Sample size too small to report data reliably.
The ratios are calculated by dividing the later year's estimate by the earlier year's estimate. The ratio is useful in comparing trends across states.

Table 14. Trend in Number of Dove Hunters, by State of Activity: 1991–2006
(in 000's)

	1991	1996	2001	2006	2006–1991 Ratio	2006–2001 Ratio
U.S. Total	**1,851**	**1,581**	**1,450**	**1,238**	**0.7**	**0.9**
Alabama	96	68	72	59	0.6	0.8
Alaska	...	...	...	...	N.A.	N.A.
Arizona	68	69	50	32	0.5	0.6
Arkansas	41	45	36	24	0.6	0.7
California	161	159	...	108	0.7	N.A.
Colorado	28	23	...	...	N.A.	N.A.
Connecticut	...	...	...	...	N.A.	N.A.
Delaware	7	13	...	3	0.4	N.A.
Florida	60	...	...	...	N.A.	N.A.
Georgia	68	117	75	97	1.4	1.3
Hawaii	...	...	...	...	N.A.	N.A.
Idaho	10	...	...	...	N.A.	N.A.
Illinois	59	53	...	30	0.5	N.A.
Indiana	25	...	...	...	N.A.	N.A.
Iowa	...	...	...	...	N.A.	N.A.
Kansas	46	41	50	34	0.7	0.7
Kentucky	63	54	49	...	N.A.	N.A.
Louisiana	70	58	24	38	0.5	1.6
Maine	...	...	...	...	N.A.	N.A.
Maryland	22	...	...	...	N.A.	N.A.
Massachusetts	...	...	...	...	N.A.	N.A.
Michigan	...	...	...	...	N.A.	N.A.
Minnesota	...	...	...	...	N.A.	N.A.
Mississippi	58	85	38	26	0.4	0.7
Missouri	52	40	34	54	1.0	1.6
Montana	...	...	...	...	N.A.	N.A.
Nebraska	30	19	13	17	0.6	1.3
Nevada	12	8	12	...	N.A.	N.A.
New Hampshire	...	...	...	...	N.A.	N.A.
New Jersey	...	...	...	...	N.A.	N.A.
New Mexico	19	16	27	6	0.3	0.2
New York	...	...	...	...	N.A.	N.A.
North Carolina	79	89	92	...	N.A.	N.A.
North Dakota	6	...	6	...	N.A.	N.A.
Ohio	...	...	...	...	N.A.	N.A.
Oklahoma	62	48	59	37	0.6	0.6
Oregon	...	...	...	...	N.A.	N.A.
Pennsylvania	74	...	...	...	N.A.	N.A.
Rhode Island	...	...	...	...	N.A.	N.A.
South Carolina	57	71	51	28	0.5	0.5
South Dakota	13	13	9	...	N.A.	N.A.
Tennessee	60	50	69	54	0.9	0.8
Texas	412	291	461	394	1.0	0.9
Utah	12	12	21	13	1.1	0.6
Vermont	...	...	...	...	N.A.	N.A.
Virginia	78	32	38	38	0.5	1.0
Washington	...	...	...	...	N.A.	N.A.
West Virginia	...	...	...	...	N.A.	N.A.
Wisconsin	...	...	...	...	N.A.	N.A.
Wyoming	...	...	...	...	N.A.	N.A.

Note: the 2001–2006 U.S. total difference is not statistically significant.
N.A. Not available   ... Sample size too small to report data reliably.
The ratios are calculated by dividing the later year's estimate by the earlier year's estimate. The ratio is useful in comparing trends across states.

Fishing days

An additional method of looking at species fishing and hunting is analyzing days afield. This gives us a measure of the effort of the participants. If the average angler changes his/her level of effort, the same number of anglers from one year to the next can contribute more (or less) days.

There was no significant difference in aggregate fishing days when comparing 1991 to 2006, although from 2001 to 2006 days decreased significantly. Bass, trout, catfish and freshwater anything fishing days showed no significant difference from 1991 to 2006 (although freshwater anything did undergo a significant decrease from 2001 to 2006). As for the saltwater species, flatfishing and saltwater anything days had no significant difference for the 1991–2006 time span. All species fishing days followed the aggregate fishing days trend of no significant difference for the 1991–2006 comparison. However, of this report's selected species, only freshwater anything days followed the overall downward trend from 2001 to 2006. In an aside from this report's focus species, walleye, sauger, and steelhead days tended down, but not significantly, while salmon fishing days dropped significantly from 2001 to 2006.

Table 15. Trend In Days of Fishing and Hunting by Species: 1991–2006
(U.S. Totals. Totals in thousands)

| | 1991 | 1996 | 2001 | 2006 | Average Days | | | |
					1991	1996	2001	2006
Total fishing days	**511,329**	**625,893**	**557,394**	**516,781**	**14**	**18**	**16**	**17**
Bass	162,595	196,385	166,202	163,924	12	15	15	16
Trout	86,626	97,978	89,285	82,143	9	11	11	12
Catfish	96,451	91,498	103,664	98,190	10	12	14	14
Freshwater anything	40,558	41,280	48,251	37,135	8	9	10	9
Flatfish	16,170	28,644	21,111	20,478	7	11	9	10
Saltwater anything	17,861	24,807	25,240	20,774	6	8	8	9
Total hunting days	**235,806**	**256,676**	**228,368**	**219,925**	**17**	**18**	**18**	**18**
Deer	112,853	131,345	133,457	132,194	11	12	13	13
Turkey	13,483	18,532	23,165	25,828	8	8	9	10
Duck	8,800	13,800	18,290	12,173	8	9	12	11
Dove	9,480	8,141	9,041	5,893	5	5	6	5
Squirrel	29,602	25,401	22,333	18,534	8	8	11	10
Rabbit	35,624	28,873	22,768	20,513	9	9	11	11

Figure 12. Freshwater Fishing Days Trend

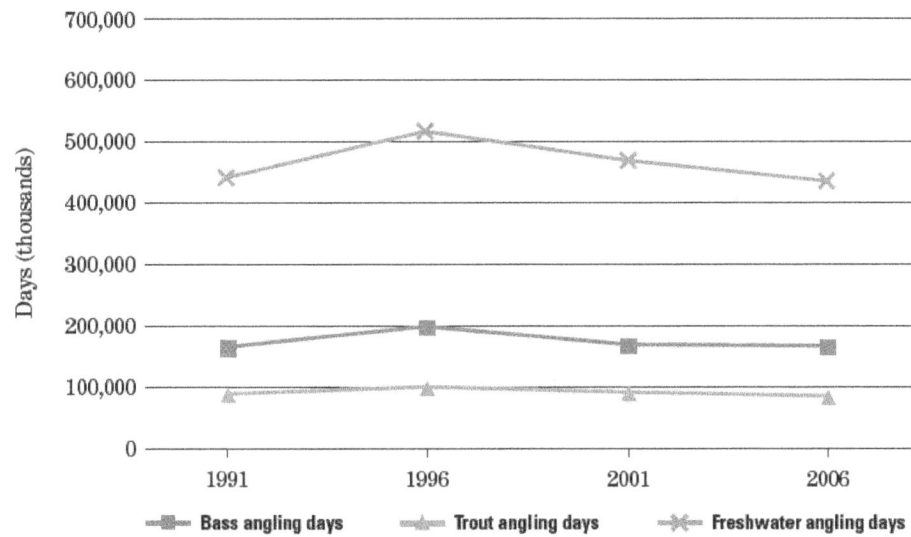

Figure 13. Indexed Freshwater Fishing Days Trend

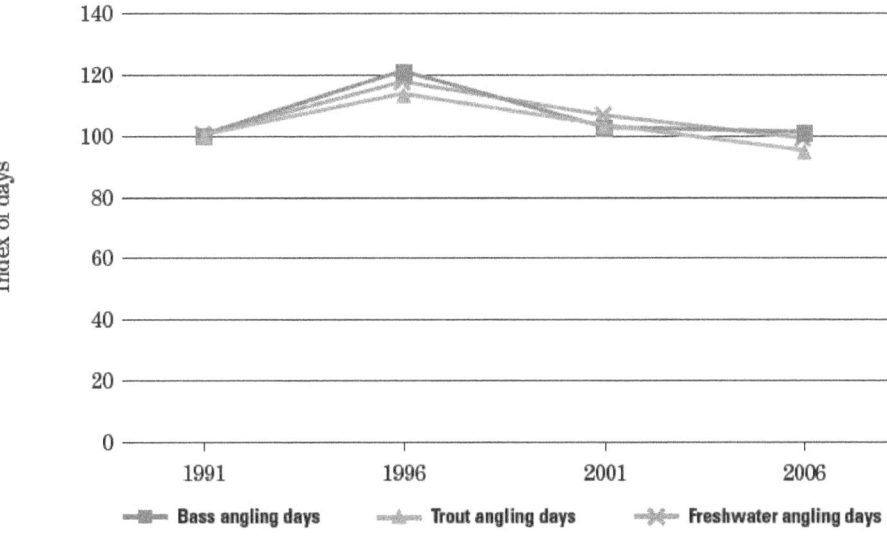

Figure 14. Freshwater Fishing Days Trend

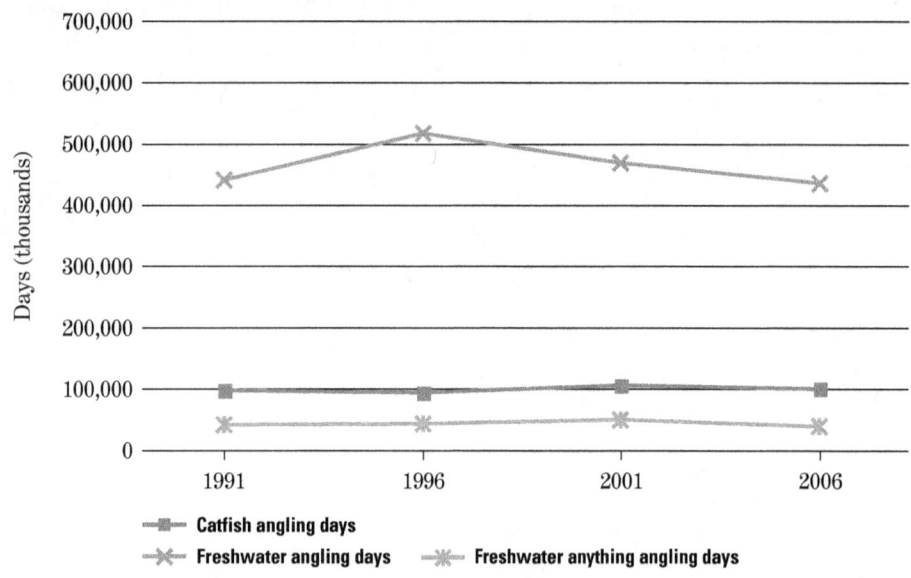

Figure 15. Indexed Freshwater Fishing Days Trend

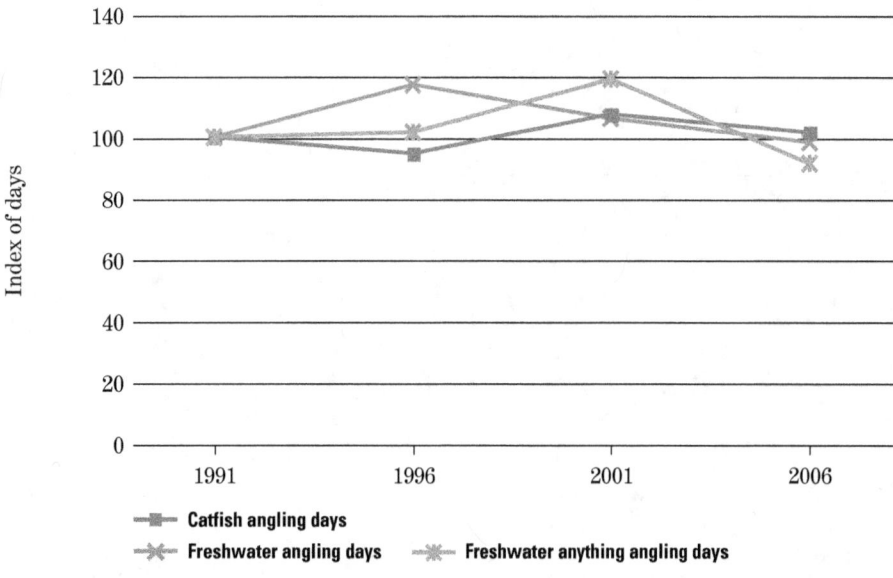

Figure 16. Saltwater Fishing Days Trend

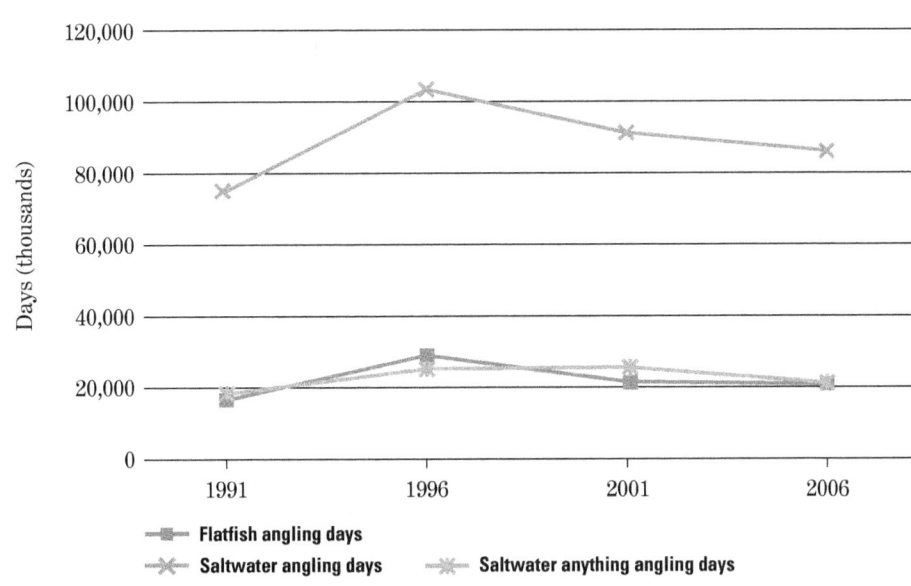

Figure 17. Indexed Saltwater Fishing Days Trend

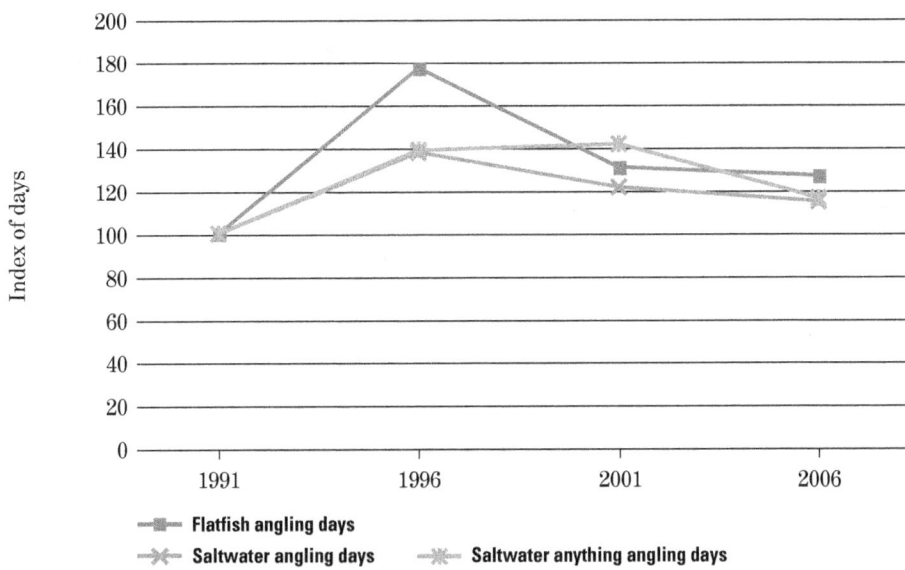

Hunting days

Similar to fishing days, there was no significant difference in the number of aggregate hunting days for the 1991–2006 comparison. Unlike fishing days, there was no significant difference for the 2001–2006 time span. Deer and turkey days saw a significant increase 1991–2006 and no significant difference 2001–2006. Duck days had a significant increase for 1991–2006 and a significant decrease for 2001–2006. Dove days had a significant decrease for 1991–2006 and 2001–2006. Rabbit and squirrel days underwent a significant decrease for 1991–2006 and no significant difference 2001–2006. The deer/turkey/duck hunting days' 1991–2006 increase counteracted the dove/rabbit/squirrel days' decrease. All but duck and dove hunting days (which decreased) followed the overall trend (no change) for 2001–2006.

Figure 18. Big Game Hunting Day Trend

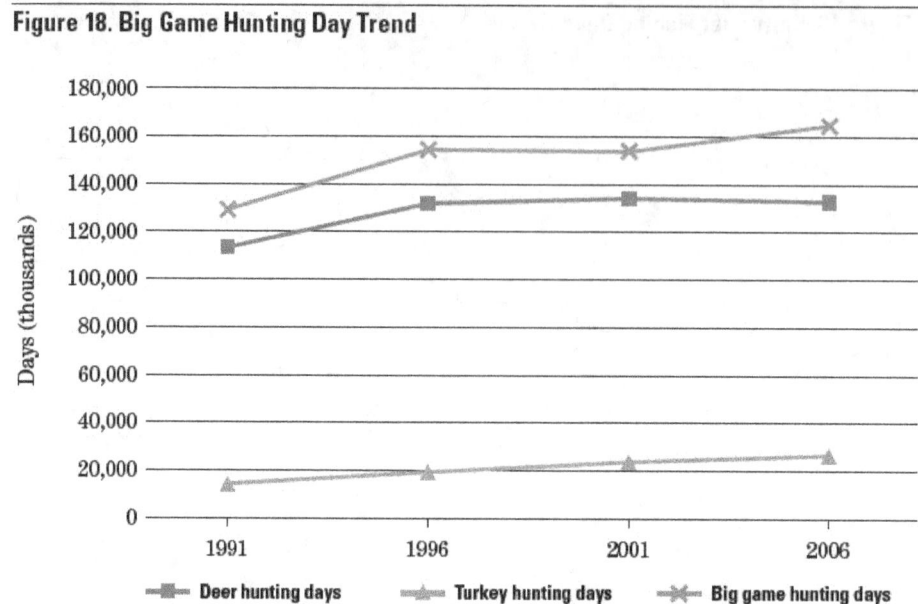

Figure 19. Indexed Big Game Hunting Day Trend

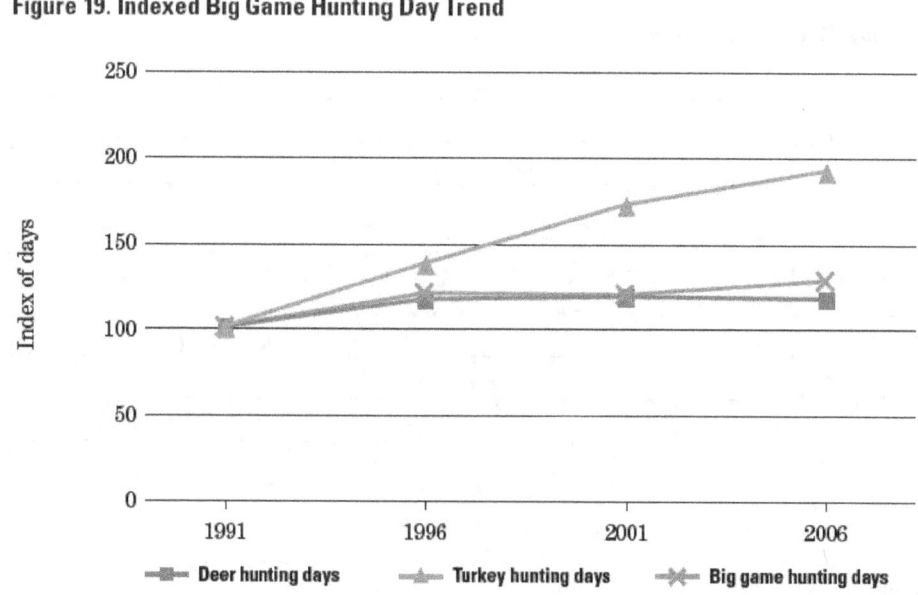

Figure 20. Small Game Hunting Days Trend

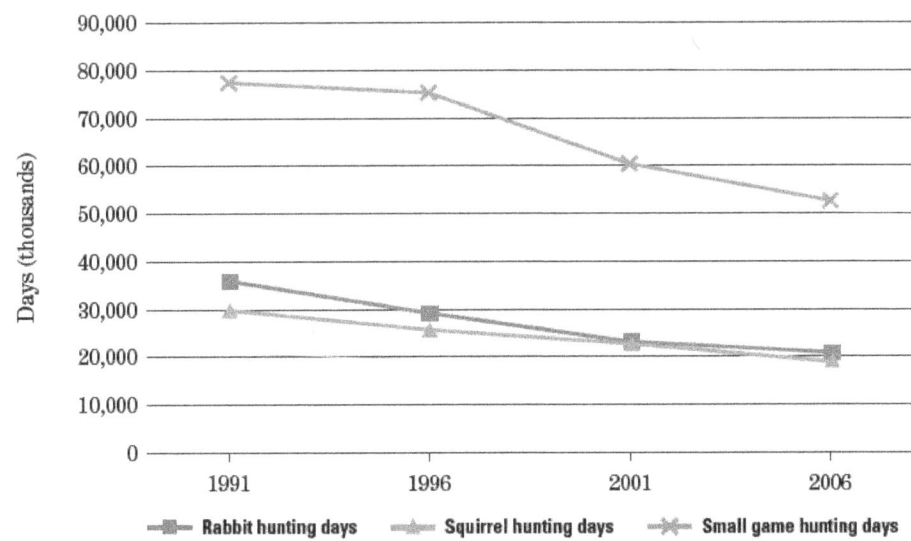

Figure 21. Indexed Small Game Hunting Days Trend

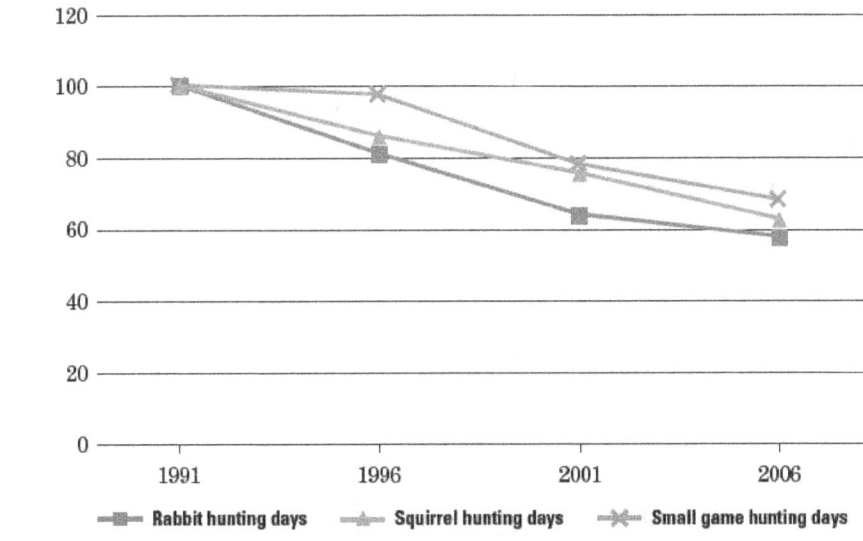

Figure 22. Migratory Bird Hunting Days Trend

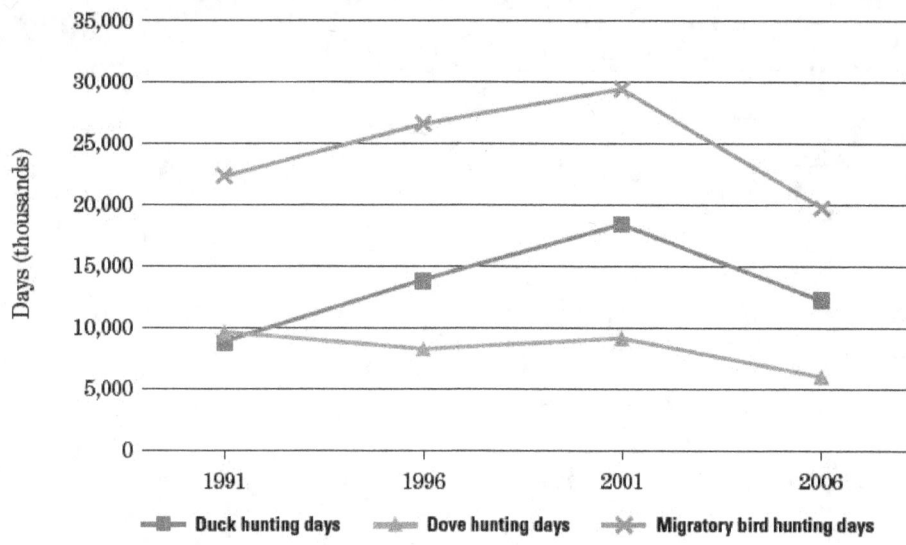

Figure 23. Indexed Migratory Bird Hunting Days Trend

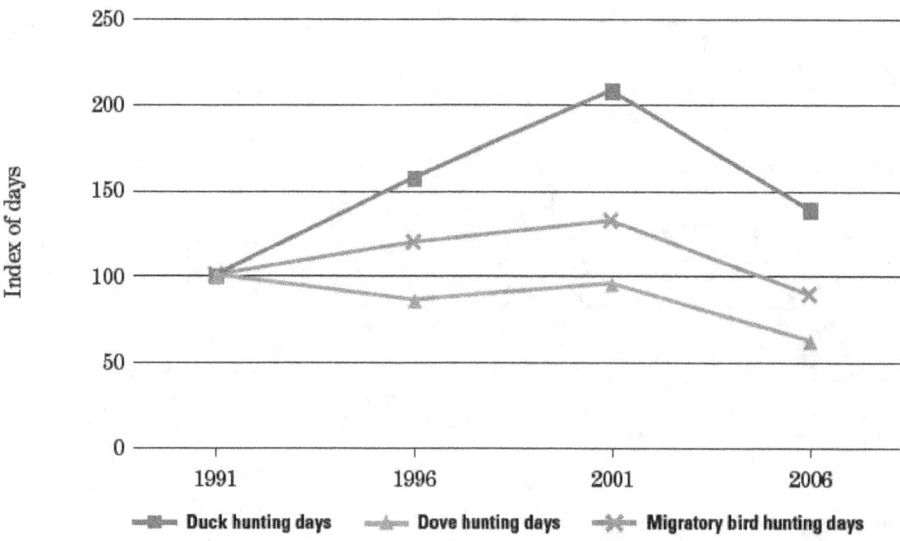

Fishing Expenditures

Aggregate fishing expenditures increased a third from 1991 to 1996, fell a fifth from 1996 to 2001, and rose slightly from 2001 to 2006. Comparing 2006 to 1991 expenditures finds an 18% increase in inflation-adjusted dollars. Fishing expenditures for all of this report's selected species increased from 1991 to 1996, but there was not as much similarity with aggregate fishing expenditures after that. Bass, trout, and catfish angling expenditures mirrored the aggregate trend. Freshwater anything, saltwater anything, and flatfish angling expenditures declined from 1996 to 2006.

Table 16. Trend in Trip and Equipment Hunting and Fishing Expenditures by Species: 1991–2006
(U.S. totals. Dollars adjusted for inflation.)

	1991 (thousands of dollars)	1996 (thousands of dollars)	2001 (thousands of dollars)	2006 (thousands of dollars)	Averages			
					1991 (dollars)	1996 (dollars)	2001 (dollars)	2006 (dollars)
Fishing								
Bass	4,720,032	7,451,326	5,028,546	5,673,291	359	574	459	557
Trout	2,514,699	3,717,524	2,701,374	2,842,910	265	400	333	405
Catfish	2,799,913	3,471,657	3,136,419	3,398,285	305	467	417	489
Freshwater anything	1,177,374	1,566,264	1,459,864	1,285,216	223	350	300	312
Flatfish	1,041,692	1,949,511	1,270,560	1,245,751	453	742	560	602
Saltwater anything	1,150,628	1,688,365	1,519,063	1,263,758	406	570	488	521
Hunting								
Deer	6,183,360	9,871,898	8,956,092	8,904,846	602	921	872	885
Turkey	738,751	1,392,866	1,554,567	1,739,825	430	636	621	677
Duck	336,768	704,279	735,551	653,633	289	441	463	570
Dove	362,791	415,474	363,593	316,426	196	263	251	256
Squirrel	604,481	832,118	576,807	625,194	169	259	272	339
Rabbit	727,452	945,858	588,042	691,950	183	301	280	360

Figure 24. Freshwater Fishing Trip and Equipment Expenditures Trend

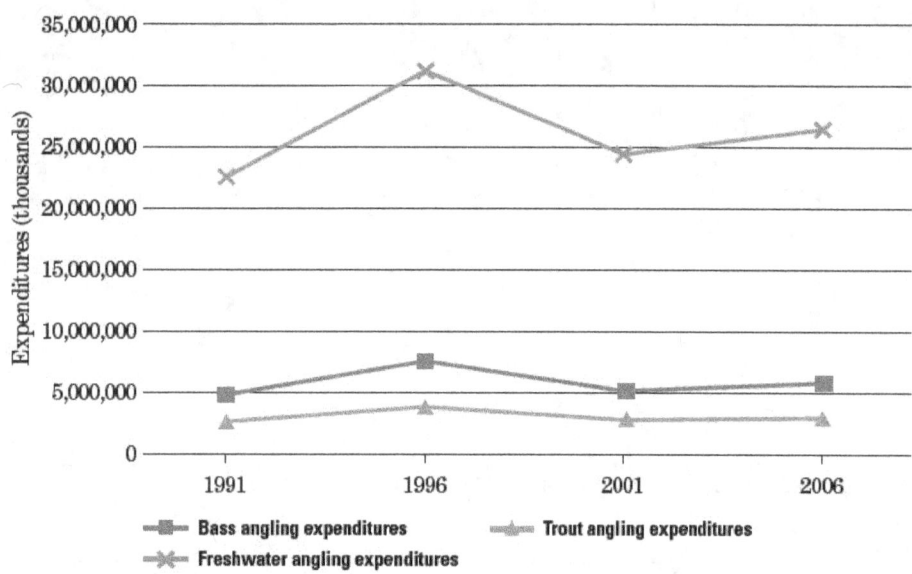

Figure 25. Indexed Freshwater Fishing Trip and Equipment Expenditures Trend

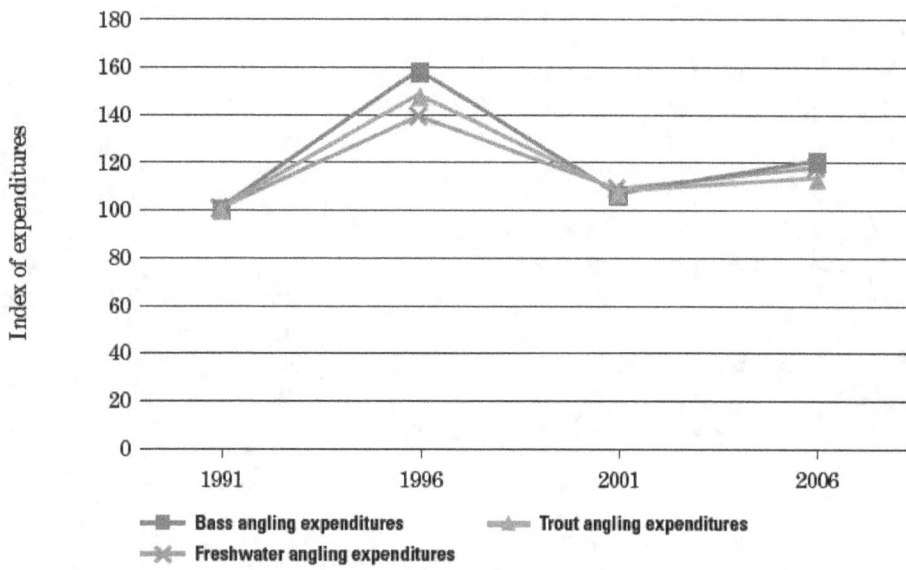

Figure 26. Freshwater Fishing Trip and Equipment Expenditures Trend

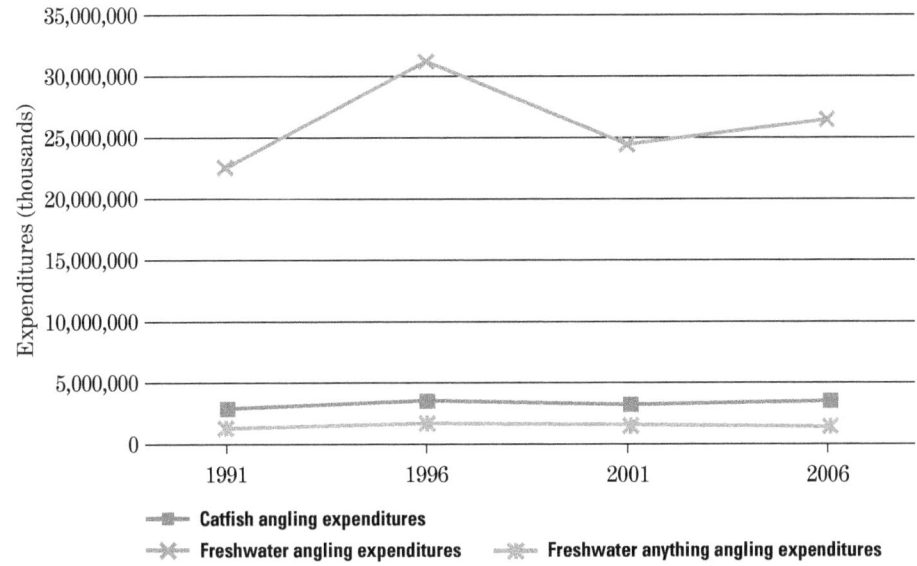

Figure 27. Indexed Freshwater Fishing Trip and Equipment Expenditures Trend

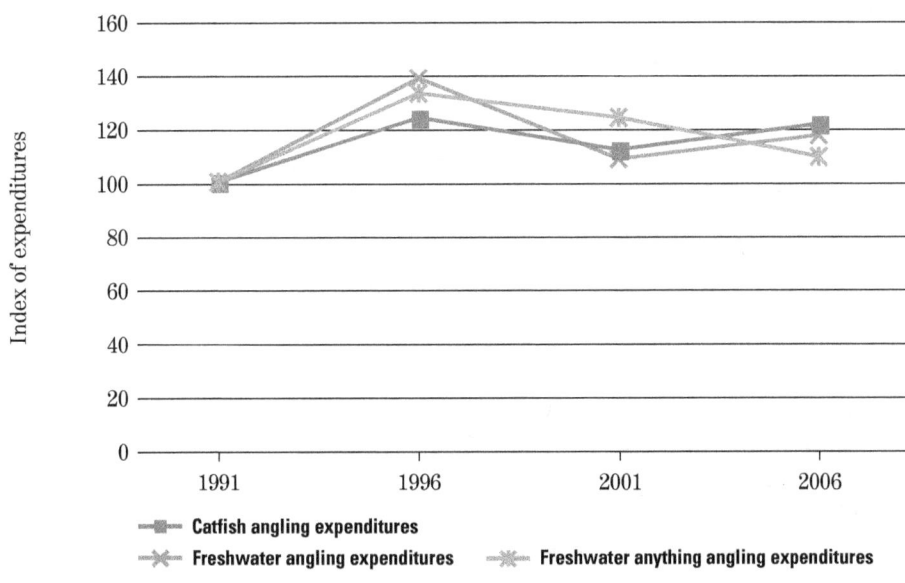

Figure 28. Saltwater Fishing Trip and Equipment Expenditures Trend

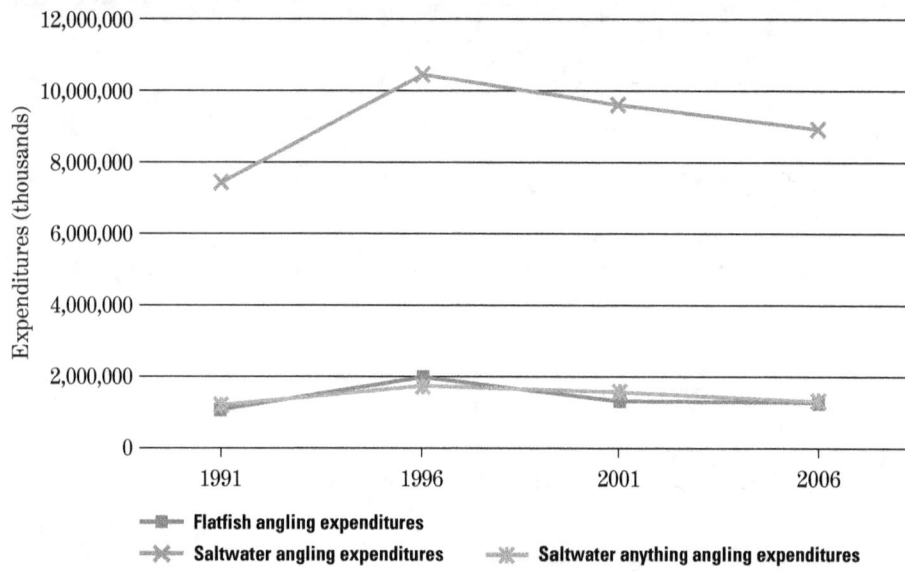

Figure 29. Indexed Saltwater Fishing Trip and Equipment Trend

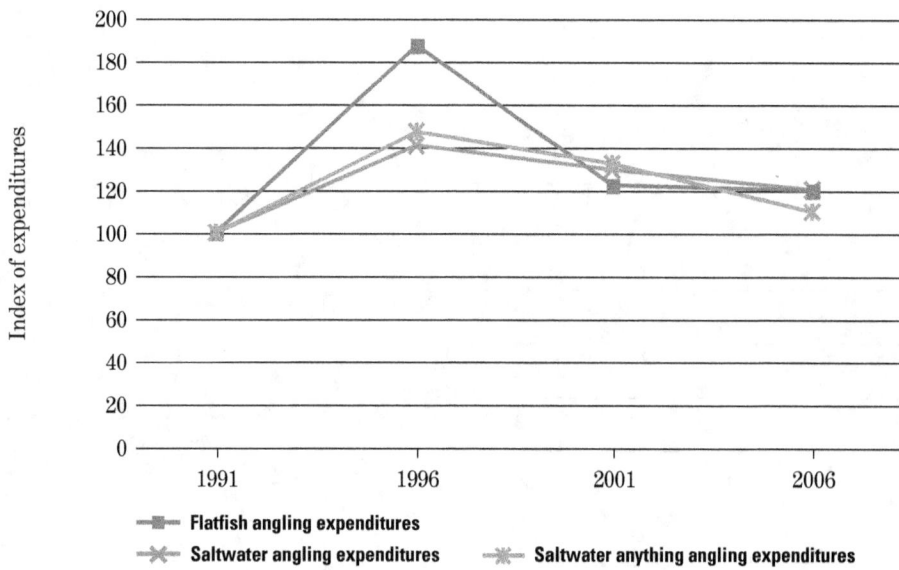

Hunting Expenditures

Aggregate hunting expenditures increased 43% from 1991 to 1996, fell 10% from 1996 to 2001, and were level from 2001 to 2006. The comparison of 1991 and 2006 reveals a 23% increase. As with fishing, all species hunting expenditures increased from 1991 to 1996, but there was no consistency after that. Deer hunting expenditures followed the aggregate trend. Turkey hunting expenditures increased steadily from 1991 to 2006 (more than doubling). Duck hunting expenditures increased from 1991 to 2001 then declined 10% from 2001 to 2006. Dove hunting expenditures decreased steadily from 1996 to 2006 (a 24% decrease). Squirrel and rabbit hunting expenditures increased from 1991 to 1996, decreased from 1996 to 2001, and increased from 2001 to 2006. The 1991 to 2006 comparison reveals no change for both squirrel and rabbit hunting expenditures.

Figure 30. Big Game Hunting Trip and Equipment Expenditures Trend

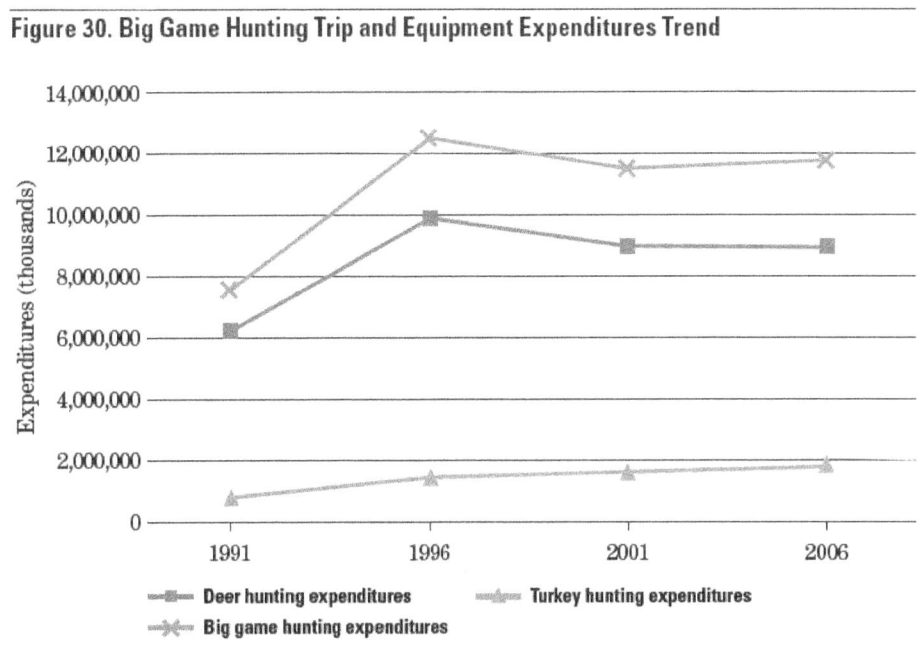

Figure 31. Indexed Big Game Hunting Trip and Equipment Expenditures Trend

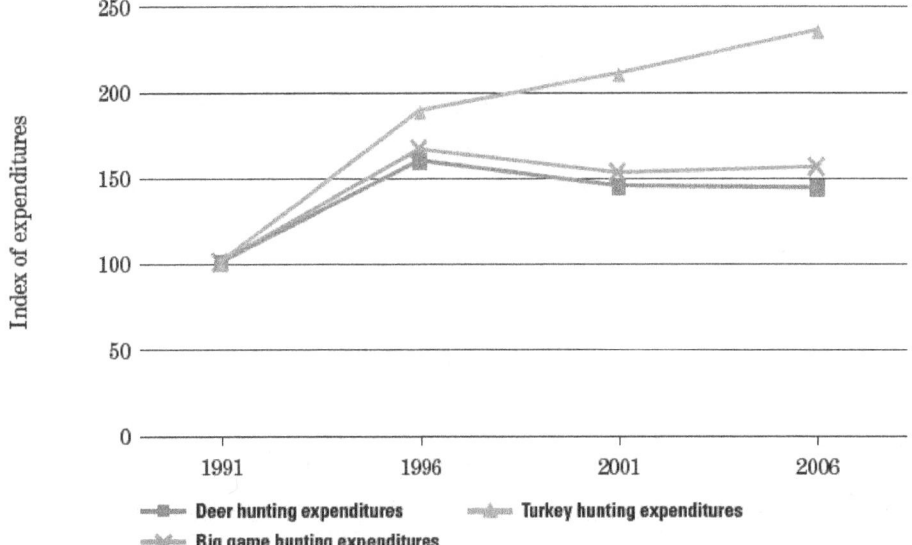

Figure 32. Small Game Hunting Trip and Equipment Expenditures Trend

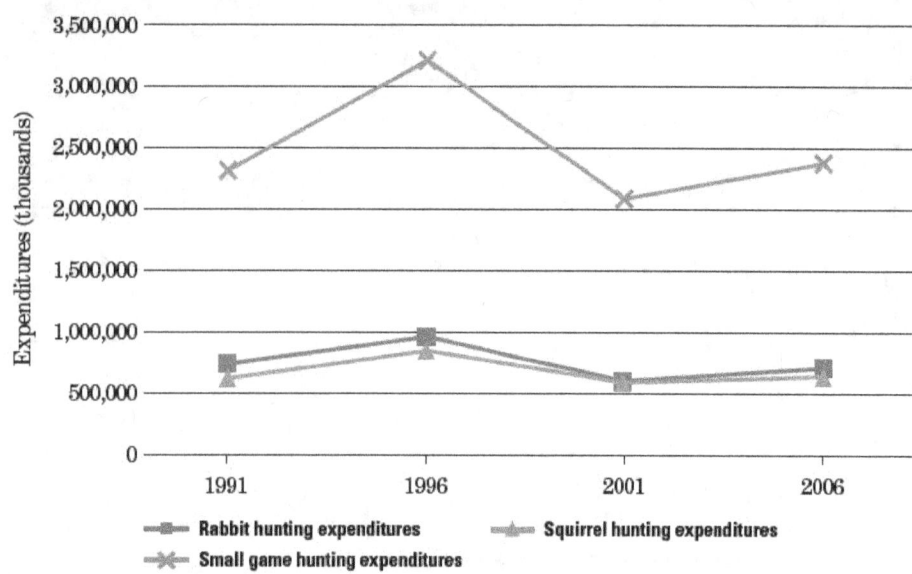

Figure 33. Indexed Small Game Hunting Trip and Equipment Expenditures Trend

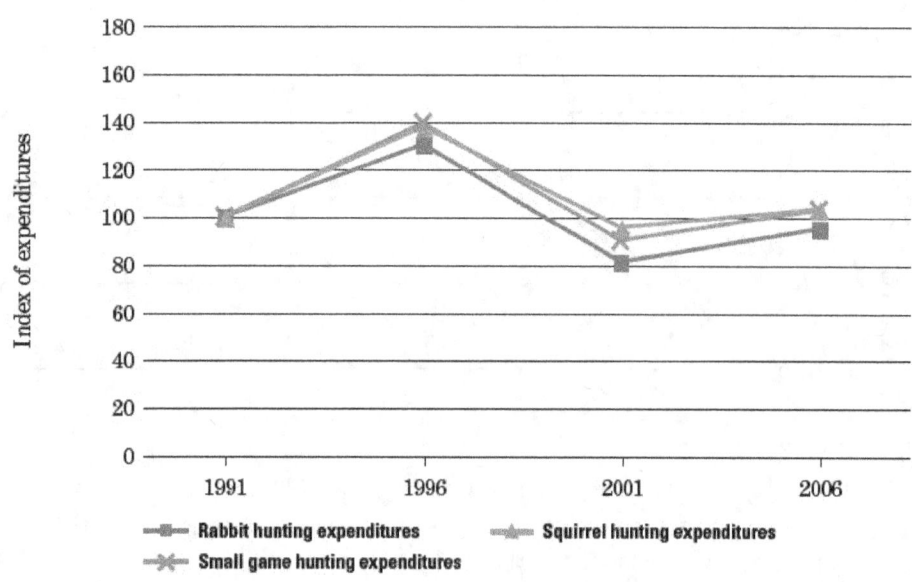

Figure 34. Migratory Bird Hunting Trip and Equipment Expenditures Trend

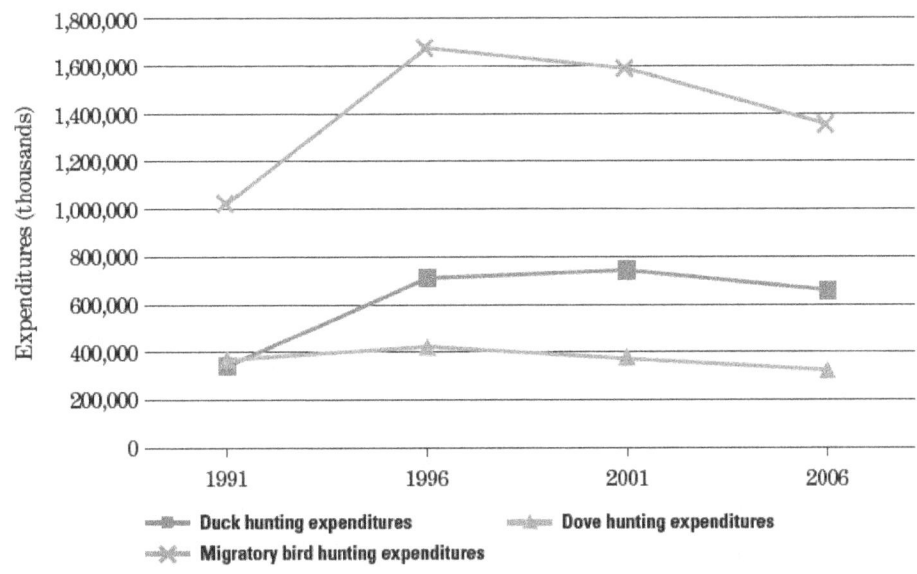

Figure 35. Indexed Migratory Bird Hunting Trip and Equipment Expenditures Trend

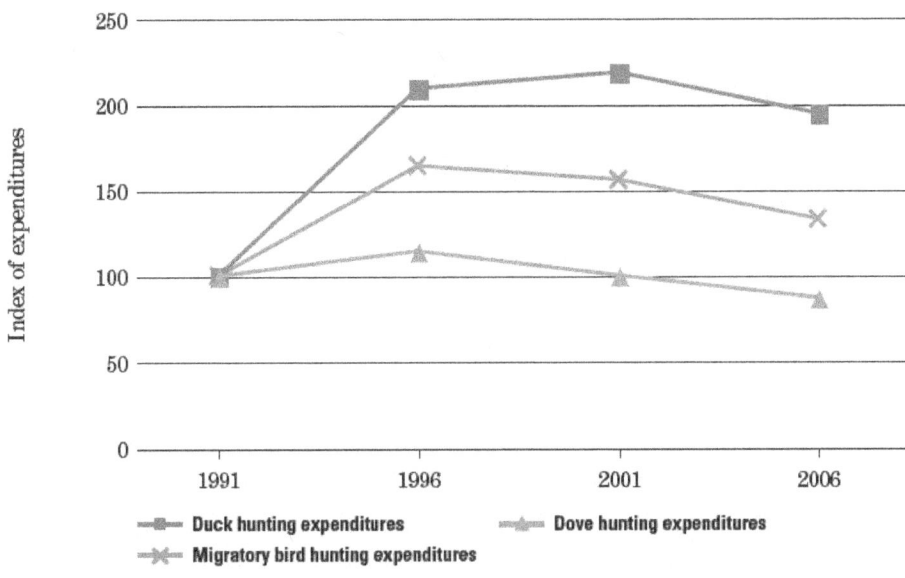

State Participation Trends

National trends are interesting and important, but the requisite data aggregation masks regional variation. Analyzing state estimates gives insight into who is doing what and where.

The tool used here to measure state trends is the participation rate of state residents. (The denominator of the participation rate calculation is the state population, so state resident participants has to be used as the numerator. There is no easy way to calculate participation rates for in-state participants.) Participation rates are the proportion of state residents that participate in an activity. They are a good measure of the popularity of an activity among the general population, plus it is easy to compare them across states. Using participation rates removes the disparity in population levels among the states from the comparison.

Hunting Participation Rates
The aggregate participation rate for deer hunting was 5% in 1991, 1996, and 2001, then fell to 4% in 2006. Twenty-six states had above average deer hunting participation rates in 2006 (Alabama, Arkansas, Idaho, Iowa, Kansas, Louisiana, Maine, Michigan, Minnesota, Mississippi, Missouri, Montana, North Dakota, Ohio, Oklahoma, Oregon, Pennsylvania, South Dakota, Tennessee, Texas, Utah, Vermont, Virginia, West Virginia, Wisconsin, and Wyoming). The five states with the highest participation rates were Montana, North Dakota, Wisconsin, Maine, and West Virginia. The state with the lowest rate was California.

Figure 36. The State Participation Rates of Deer Hunters Relative to the National Participation Rate: 2006

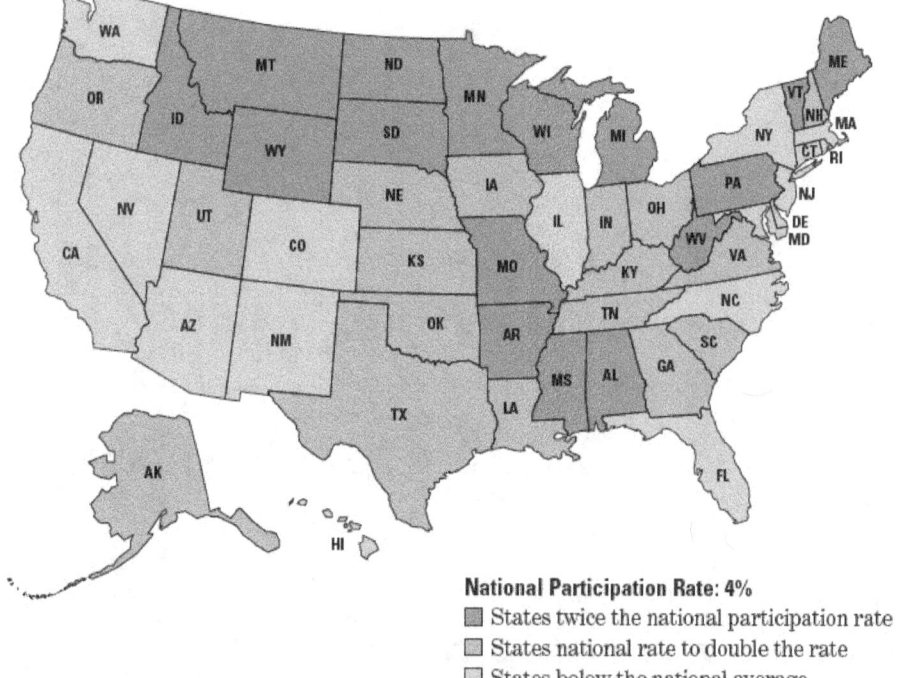

National Participation Rate: 4%
- ▣ States twice the national participation rate
- ▩ States national rate to double the rate
- ▢ States below the national average

Table 17. Trend in Number of Deer Hunters, by State of Residence: 1991–2006
(Numbers in thousands)

	Number of participants				Participation rates			
	1991	1996	2001	2006	1991	1996	2001	2006
U.S. Total	10,277	10,722	10,272	10,062	5	5	5	4
Alabama	219	212	293	284	7	6	9	8
Alaska	9	17	18	20	2	4	4	4
Arizona	94	72	65	70	3	2	2	2
Arkansas	217	268	278	268	12	14	14	12
California	235	298	93	131	1	1	(Z)	(Z)
Colorado	108	144	72	41	4	5	2	1
Connecticut	36	51	34	29	1	2	1	1
Delaware	17	27	12	17	3	5	2	3
Florida	265	161	242	252	3	1	2	2
Georgia	259	299	307	305	5	5	5	4
Hawaii	7	11	8	9	1	1	1	1
Idaho	132	152	108	92	18	17	11	8
Illinois	277	286	252	176	3	3	3	2
Indiana	200	263	200	208	5	6	4	4
Iowa	141	178	131	164	7	8	6	7
Kansas	67	97	111	88	4	5	6	4
Kentucky	184	255	201	215	7	8	6	7
Louisiana	213	254	214	211	7	8	6	6
Maine	117	135	115	138	12	14	11	13
Maryland	114	97	106	127	3	2	3	3
Massachusetts	97	82	68	59	2	2	1	1
Michigan	713	800	640	696	10	11	8	9
Minnesota	332	463	467	410	10	13	13	10
Mississippi	248	257	221	234	13	13	10	11
Missouri	352	406	339	453	9	10	8	10
Montana	134	117	132	125	22	17	19	17
Nebraska	61	75	73	61	5	6	6	4
Nevada	32	29	24	26	4	2	2	1
New Hampshire	57	54	46	45	7	6	5	4
New Jersey	106	78	112	61	2	1	2	1
New Mexico	58	56	62	26	5	4	5	2
New York	613	552	578	464	4	4	4	3
North Carolina	289	258	221	226	6	5	4	3
North Dakota	60	61	77	72	13	13	16	14
Ohio	379	296	417	404	5	3	5	5
Oklahoma	127	218	192	180	5	9	7	7
Oregon	190	215	177	159	9	9	7	6
Pennsylvania	836	703	825	892	9	8	9	9
Rhode Island	13	16	8	11	2	2	1	1
South Carolina	139	200	191	135	5	7	6	4
South Dakota	60	56	51	54	11	10	9	9
Tennessee	214	236	201	223	6	6	5	5
Texas	713	703	857	774	6	5	6	5
Utah	137	90	128	95	12	6	8	5
Vermont	65	65	70	54	15	14	15	11
Virginia	293	324	270	310	6	6	5	5
Washington	180	210	169	156	5	5	4	3
West Virginia	237	236	208	186	17	16	14	13
Wisconsin	599	527	547	594	16	14	13	14
Wyoming	49	44	40	31	14	12	11	8

(Z) Less than 0.5 percent.

The aggregate participation rate for turkey hunting was 1% in every survey year. Eighteen states had above average turkey hunting participation rates in 2006 (Alabama, Arkansas, Iowa, Kansas, Kentucky, Louisiana, Maine, Mississippi, Missouri, Nebraska, Oklahoma, Pennsylvania, South Carolina, Tennessee, Vermont, Virginia, West Virginia, and Wisconsin). The states with the highest rates were Arkansas, Pennsylvania, Wisconsin, Mississippi, Missouri, Vermont, and West Virginia. The states with the lowest rate (for states which have estimates) were California and New Jersey.

Figure 37. The State Participation Rates of Turkey Hunters Relative to the National Participation Rate: 2006

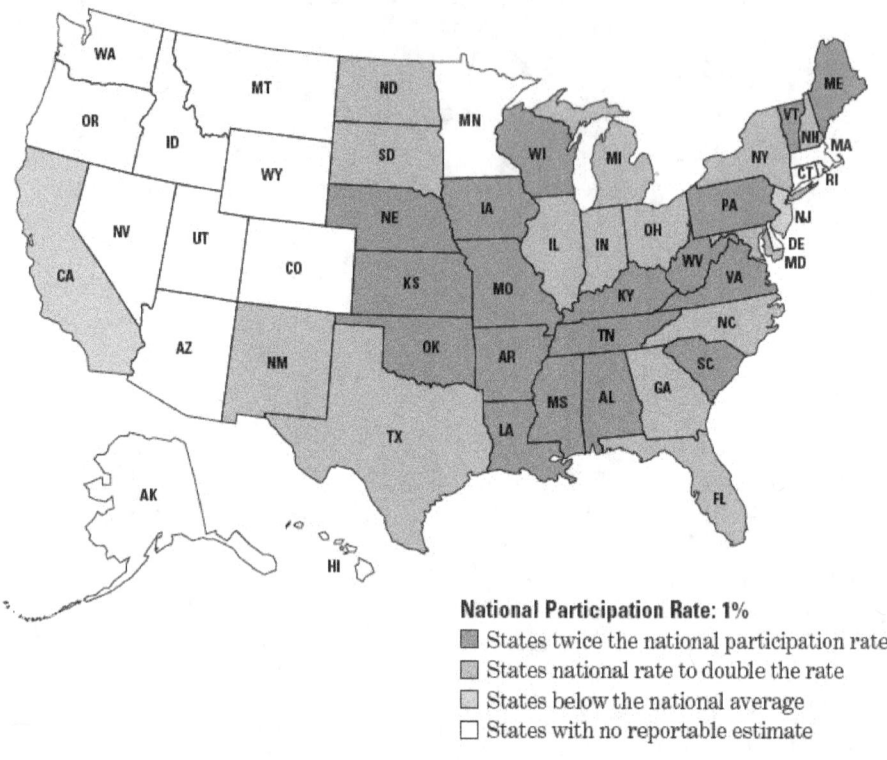

National Participation Rate: 1%
- ▓ States twice the national participation rate
- ▒ States national rate to double the rate
- ░ States below the national average
- ☐ States with no reportable estimate

Table 18. Trend in Number of Turkey Hunters, by State of Residence: 1991–2006
(Numbers in thousands)

	Number of participants				Participation rates			
	1991	1996	2001	2006	1991	1996	2001	2006
U.S. Total	**1,720**	**2,189**	**2,504**	**2,569**	**1**	**1**	**1**	**1**
Alabama	58	45	54	86	2	1	2	2
Alaska	...	...	...	...	N.A.	N.A.	N.A.	N.A.
Arizona	...	...	...	...	N.A.	N.A.	N.A.	N.A.
Arkansas	31	67	105	82	2	4	5	4
California	...	...	...	48	N.A.	N.A.	N.A.	(Z)
Colorado	...	...	...	...	N.A.	N.A.	N.A.	N.A.
Connecticut	...	10	...	...	N.A.	(Z)	N.A.	N.A.
Delaware	...	4	...	...	...	1	...	...
Florida	47	...	105	85	(Z)	...	1	1
Georgia	46	67	77	72	1	1	1	1
Hawaii	...	...	...	...	N.A.	N.A.	N.A.	N.A.
Idaho	...	...	...	...	N.A.	N.A.	N.A.	N.A.
Illinois	28	53	57	67	(Z)	1	1	1
Indiana	19	...	47	33	(Z)	...	1	1
Iowa	20	41	24	51	1	2	1	2
Kansas	16	25	48	47	1	1	2	2
Kentucky	21	73	97	63	1	2	3	2
Louisiana	22	...	26	56	1	...	1	2
Maine	...	...	10	18	...	...	1	2
Maryland	25	...	21	26	1	...	1	1
Massachusetts	15	19	...	...	(Z)	(Z)	N.A.	N.A.
Michigan	37	...	68	78	1	...	1	1
Minnesota	...	...	...	...	N.A.	N.A.	N.A.	N.A.
Mississippi	51	68	72	56	3	3	3	3
Missouri	125	149	139	140	3	4	3	3
Montana	...	...	...	...	N.A.	N.A.	N.A.	N.A.
Nebraska	14	10	15	23	1	1	1	2
Nevada	...	...	...	...	N.A.	N.A.	N.A.	N.A.
New Hampshire	...	7	11	10	...	1	1	1
New Jersey	...	...	24	20	N.A.	N.A.	(Z)	(Z)
New Mexico	12	...	13	20	1	...	1	1
New York	126	209	269	144	1	1	2	1
North Carolina	32	49	60	82	1	1	1	1
North Dakota	3	...	...	7	1	...	...	1
Ohio	30	79	98	97	(Z)	1	1	1
Oklahoma	29	56	72	66	1	2	3	2
Oregon	...	...	16	...	...	...	1	...
Pennsylvania	314	309	272	343	3	3	3	4
Rhode Island	...	...	...	...	N.A.	N.A.	N.A.	N.A.
South Carolina	31	45	48	51	1	2	2	2
South Dakota	6	9	6	6	1	2	1	1
Tennessee	31	39	69	110	1	1	2	2
Texas	175	...	120	169	1	...	1	1
Utah	...	...	...	...	N.A.	N.A.	N.A.	N.A.
Vermont	10	8	17	13	2	2	4	3
Virginia	154	164	85	116	3	3	2	2
Washington	...	...	17	...	N.A.	N.A.	(Z)	N.A.
West Virginia	85	88	68	43	6	6	5	3
Wisconsin	49	93	116	155	1	2	3	4
Wyoming	...	...	6	...	...	...	2	...

... Sample size too small to report data reliably.
N.A. Not available   (Z) Less than 0.5 percent.

The aggregate participation rate for squirrel hunting was 2% in 1991 and 1996 and 1% in 2001 and 2006. Eight states had above average participation rates in 2006 (Alabama, Arkansas, Kentucky, Louisiana, Mississippi, Missouri, Pennsylvania, and West Virginia). The states with the highest rates in 2006 were West Virginia, Arkansas, Louisiana, Mississippi, and Missouri. The states with the lowest rate (for states which have estimates) were Florida, Illinois, and Texas.

Figure 38. The State Participation Rates of Squirrel Hunters Relative to the National Participation Rate: 2006

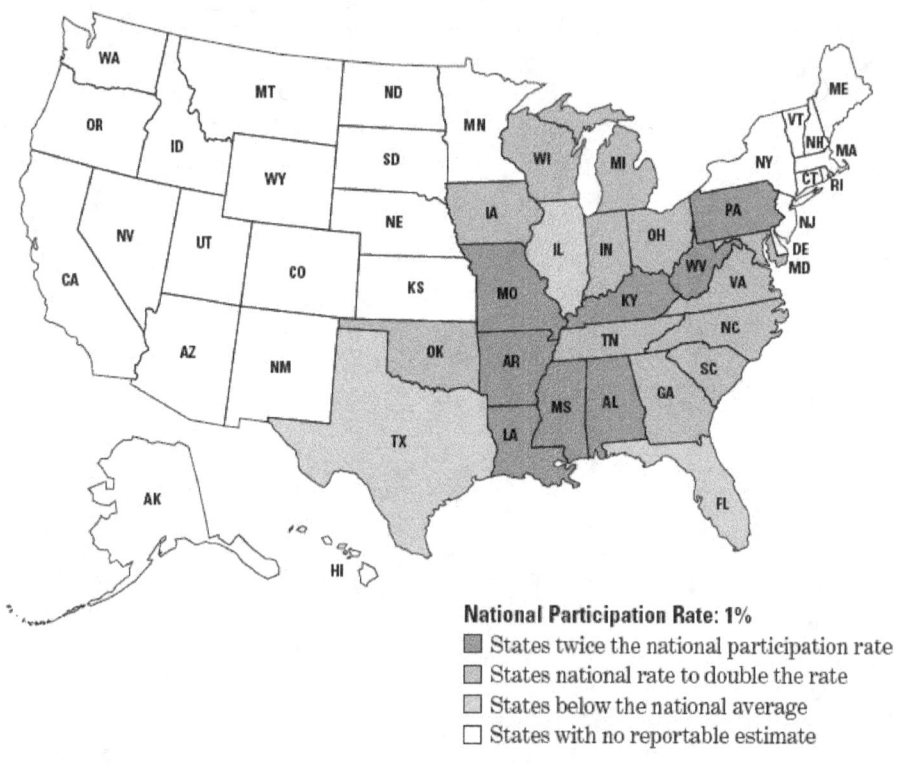

National Participation Rate: 1%

■ States twice the national participation rate
■ States national rate to double the rate
□ States below the national average
□ States with no reportable estimate

Table 19. Trend in Number of Squirrel Hunters, by State of Residence: 1991–2006
(Numbers in thousands)

	Number of participants				Participation rates			
	1991	1996	2001	2006	1991	1996	2001	2006
U.S. Total	**3,569**	**3,207**	**2,119**	**1,845**	**2**	**2**	**1**	**1**
Alabama	88	49	57	72	3	1	2	2
Alaska	...	...	...	...	N.A.	N.A.	N.A.	N.A.
Arizona	...	...	...	...	N.A.	N.A.	N.A.	N.A.
Arkansas	108	134	107	88	6	7	5	4
California	65	...	...	...	(Z)	N.A.	N.A.	N.A.
Colorado	...	...	...	...	N.A.	N.A.	N.A.	N.A.
Connecticut	8	...	...	...	(Z)	N.A.	N.A.	N.A.
Delaware	7	8	...	...	1	1	...	...
Florida	109	...	...	60	1	...	...	(Z)
Georgia	74	92	80	88	2	2	1	1
Hawaii	...	...	...	...	N.A.	N.A.	N.A.	N.A.
Idaho	12	...	...	...	2	...	...	...
Illinois	125	166	...	48	1	2	...	(Z)
Indiana	134	119	88	53	3	3	2	1
Iowa	67	69	33	24	3	3	1	1
Kansas	33	22	22	...	2	1	1	...
Kentucky	162	137	94	77	6	5	3	2
Louisiana	165	196	81	100	5	6	2	3
Maine	...	...	...	...	N.A.	N.A.	N.A.	N.A.
Maryland	52	35	21	31	1	1	1	1
Massachusetts	14	...	...	...	(Z)	N.A.	N.A.	N.A.
Michigan	181	216	93	91	3	3	1	1
Minnesota	53	...	...	...	2	...	...	...
Mississippi	141	115	91	64	7	6	4	3
Missouri	152	175	109	144	4	4	3	3
Montana	...	...	...	...	N.A.	N.A.	N.A.	N.A.
Nebraska	16	...	...	...	1	...	...	...
Nevada	...	...	...	...	N.A.	N.A.	N.A.	N.A.
New Hampshire	8	...	...	...	1	...	...	...
New Jersey	27	...	...	...	(Z)	N.A.	N.A.	N.A.
New Mexico	...	...	...	...	N.A.	N.A.	N.A.	N.A.
New York	123	128	101	...	1	1	1	...
North Carolina	151	161	73	42	3	3	1	1
North Dakota	...	...	...	...	N.A.	N.A.	N.A.	N.A.
Ohio	212	170	168	114	3	2	2	1
Oklahoma	56	76	49	29	2	3	2	1
Oregon	10	...	...	...	(Z)	N.A.	N.A.	N.A.
Pennsylvania	354	245	204	197	4	3	2	2
Rhode Island	3	...	...	...	(Z)	N.A.	N.A.	N.A.
South Carolina	49	51	52	23	2	2	2	1
South Dakota	4	...	...	...	1	...	...	...
Tennessee	174	137	117	62	5	3	3	1
Texas	152	...	...	64	1	...	...	(Z)
Utah	...	...	...	...	N.A.	N.A.	N.A.	N.A.
Vermont	8	10	12	...	2	2	3	...
Virginia	151	116	84	77	3	2	2	1
Washington	...	...	...	...	N.A.	N.A.	N.A.	N.A.
West Virginia	152	160	101	97	11	11	7	7
Wisconsin	135	142	58	60	4	4	1	1
Wyoming	...	...	...	...	N.A.	N.A.	N.A.	N.A.

... Sample size too small to report data reliably.
N.A. Not available   (Z) Less than 0.5 percent.

The aggregate participation rate for rabbit hunting was the same as squirrel hunting: 2% in 1991 and 1996, 1% in 2001 and 2006. Nine states had higher than average participation rates in 2006 (Alabama, Kentucky, Louisiana, Michigan, Mississippi, Missouri, Pennsylvania, Utah, and West Virginia). The states with the highest rates in 2006 were Louisiana and West Virginia. The states with the lowest rate (for states which have estimates) were Arizona, Maryland and Nevada.

Figure 39. The State Participation Rates of Rabbit Hunters Relative to the National Participation Rate: 2006

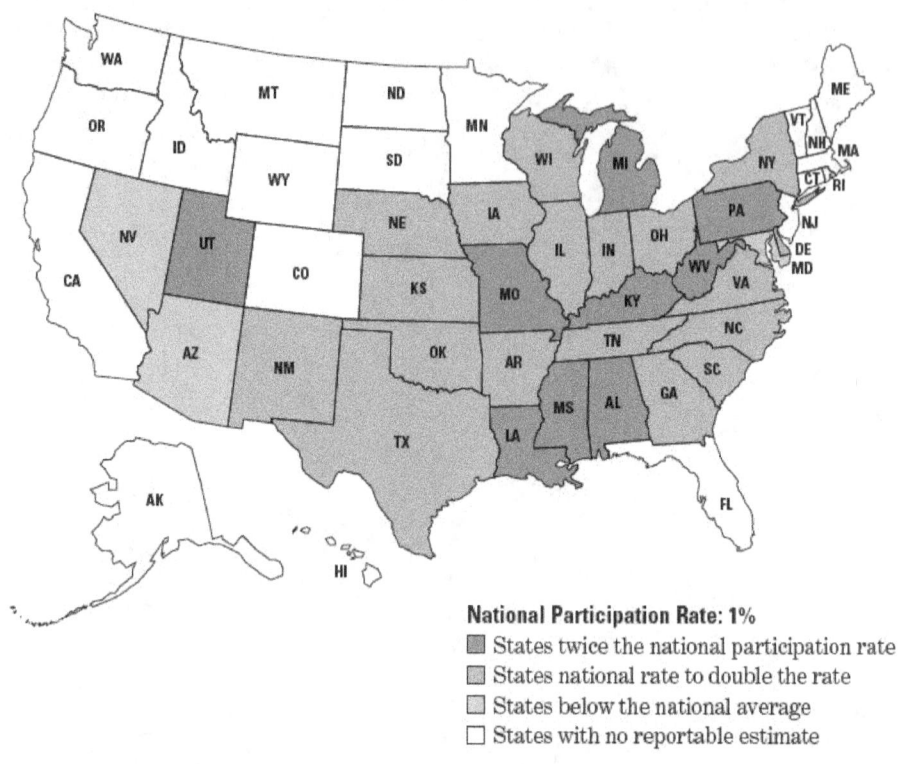

National Participation Rate: 1%
- ■ States twice the national participation rate
- ▨ States national rate to double the rate
- □ States below the national average
- □ States with no reportable estimate

Table 20. Trend in Number of Rabbit Hunters, by State of Residence: 1991–2006
(Numbers in thousands)

	Number of participants				Participation rates			
	1991	1996	2001	2006	1991	1996	2001	2006
U.S. Total	**3,980**	**3,146**	**2,099**	**1,923**	**2**	**2**	**1**	**1**
Alabama	83	31	37	58	3	1	1	2
Alaska	10	11	7	...	3	3	2	...
Arizona	20	23	21	20	1	1	1	(Z)
Arkansas	50	81	45	28	3	4	2	1
California	73	...	...	...	(Z)	N.A.	N.A.	N.A.
Colorado	35	54	23	...	1	2	1	...
Connecticut	...	...	...	...	N.A.	N.A.	N.A.	N.A.
Delaware	8	12	5	5	2	2	1	1
Florida	42	...	...	...	(Z)	N.A.	N.A.	N.A.
Georgia	68	...	53	65	1	...	1	1
Hawaii	...	...	...	...	N.A.	N.A.	N.A.	N.A.
Idaho	15	...	...	...	2	...	...	...
Illinois	166	168	...	58	2	2	...	1
Indiana	161	118	95	56	4	3	2	1
Iowa	86	97	49	32	4	4	2	1
Kansas	55	38	32	27	3	2	2	1
Kentucky	149	143	99	67	5	5	3	2
Louisiana	134	152	70	95	4	5	2	3
Maine	22	18	15	...	2	2	1	...
Maryland	42	23	24	14	1	1	1	(Z)
Massachusetts	30	...	...	...	1	...	...	...
Michigan	315	318	120	131	4	4	2	2
Minnesota	31	...	...	...	1	...	...	...
Mississippi	107	97	77	47	6	5	4	2
Missouri	155	169	93	98	4	4	2	2
Montana	11	...	...	...	2	...	...	...
Nebraska	29	16	8	11	2	1	1	1
Nevada	11	7	...	8	1	1	...	(Z)
New Hampshire	14	12	...	...	2	1	...	...
New Jersey	55	28	30	...	1	(Z)	(Z)	...
New Mexico	21	8	...	15	2	1	...	1
New York	218	172	158	98	2	1	1	1
North Carolina	108	98	62	52	2	2	1	1
North Dakota	7	...	4	...	1	...	1	...
Ohio	368	220	202	126	4	3	2	1
Oklahoma	60	61	52	29	2	2	2	1
Oregon	9	...	...	...	(Z)	N.A.	N.A.	N.A.
Pennsylvania	452	231	204	233	5	2	2	2
Rhode Island	6	4	...	...	1	1	...	...
South Carolina	39	27	42	25	1	1	1	1
South Dakota	12	10	...	...	2	2	...	...
Tennessee	126	124	65	49	3	3	2	1
Texas	140	...	...	107	1	...	...	1
Utah	43	25	28	38	4	2	2	2
Vermont	24	15	13	...	5	3	3	...
Virginia	107	59	40	72	2	1	1	1
Washington	17	...	...	...	(Z)	N.A.	N.A.	N.A.
West Virginia	79	45	45	38	6	3	3	3
Wisconsin	152	154	64	65	4	4	2	1
Wyoming	10	8	12	...	3	2	3	...

... Sample size too small to report data reliably.
N.A. Not available   (Z) Less than 0.5 percent.

The aggregate participation rate for duck hunting was 1% for every survey year. Five states had higher than average participation rates (Arkansas, Louisiana, Montana, Nebraska and North Dakota) in 2006. The state with the highest participation rate was Arkansas. The states with the lowest rate (for states which have estimates) were California, Massachusetts and Texas.

Figure 40. The State Participation Rates of Duck Hunters Relative to the National Participation Rate: 2006

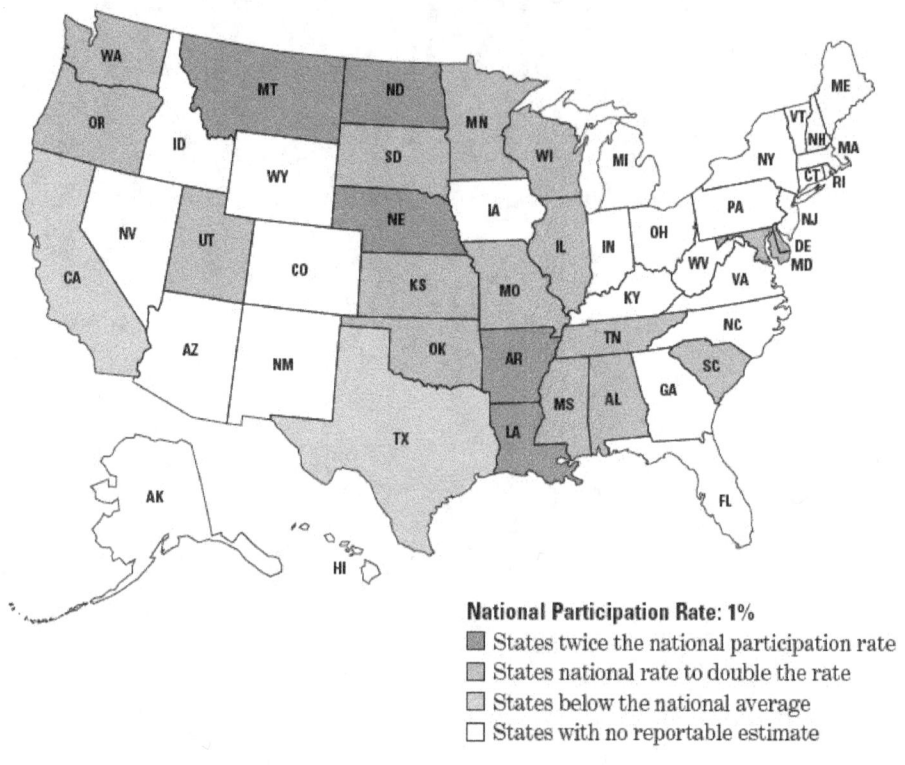

National Participation Rate: 1%
- ▨ States twice the national participation rate
- ▨ States national rate to double the rate
- ▨ States below the national average
- ☐ States with no reportable estimate

Table 21. Trend in Number of Duck Hunters, by State of Residence: 1991–2006
(Numbers in thousands)

	Number of participants				Participation rates			
	1991	1996	2001	2006	1991	1996	2001	2006
U.S. Total	**1,164**	**1,596**	**1,589**	**1,147**	**1**	**1**	**1**	**1**
Alabama	...	...	22	25	...	...	1	1
Alaska	10	10	11	...	3	2	2	...
Arizona	...	...	...	...	N.A.	N.A.	N.A.	N.A.
Arkansas	35	72	76	68	2	4	4	3
California	97	145	101	62	(Z)	1	(Z)	(Z)
Colorado	26	...	30	...	1	...	1	...
Connecticut	7	...	...	...	(Z)	N.A.	N.A.	N.A.
Delaware	8	8	3	9	2	1	1	1
Florida	...	...	...	...	N.A.	N.A.	N.A.	N.A.
Georgia	23	...	...	...	(Z)	N.A.	N.A.	N.A.
Hawaii	...	...	...	...	N.A.	N.A.	N.A.	N.A.
Idaho	17	31	18	...	2	4	2	...
Illinois	55	59	55	61	1	1	1	1
Indiana	11	...	...	...	(Z)	N.A.	N.A.	N.A.
Iowa	19	29	34	...	1	1	2	...
Kansas	10	...	24	23	1	...	1	1
Kentucky	14	...	...	...	(Z)	N.A.	N.A.	N.A.
Louisiana	80	91	104	66	3	3	3	2
Maine	10	...	...	...	1	...	...	...
Maryland	11	...	23	28	(Z)	...	1	1
Massachusetts	12	...	...	13	(Z)	N.A.	N.A.	(Z)
Michigan	42	...	...	...	1	...	...	...
Minnesota	64	129	160	52	2	4	4	1
Mississippi	25	51	27	32	1	3	1	1
Missouri	23	...	36	33	1	...	1	1
Montana	11	13	14	13	2	2	2	2
Nebraska	21	19	29	23	2	2	2	2
Nevada	6	10	14	...	1	1	1	...
New Hampshire	4	...	...	...	(Z)	N.A.	N.A.	N.A.
New Jersey	18	...	...	...	(Z)	N.A.	N.A.	N.A.
New Mexico	6	...	15	...	1	...	1	...
New York	33	...	...	...	(Z)	N.A.	N.A.	N.A.
North Carolina	21	...	57	...	(Z)	...	1	...
North Dakota	15	13	22	8	3	3	5	2
Ohio	29	...	43	...	(Z)	N.A.	(Z)	N.A.
Oklahoma	20	...	32	28	1	...	1	1
Oregon	23	52	29	26	1	2	1	1
Pennsylvania	35	...	48	...	(Z)	...	1	...
Rhode Island	3	...	...	...	(Z)	N.A.	N.A.	N.A.
South Carolina	26	41	21	29	1	1	1	1
South Dakota	19	23	26	9	4	4	5	1
Tennessee	18	...	66	47	(Z)	...	2	1
Texas	99	...	104	81	1	...	1	(Z)
Utah	9	20	41	20	1	1	3	1
Vermont	4	...	...	...	1	...	...	...
Virginia	15	...	...	...	(Z)	N.A.	N.A.	N.A.
Washington	37	47	36	25	1	1	1	1
West Virginia	...	...	...	...	N.A.	N.A.	N.A.	N.A.
Wisconsin	65	81	47	48	2	2	1	1
Wyoming	...	9	...	...	...	2	...	...

... Sample size too small to report data reliably.
N.A. Not available   (Z) Less than 0.5 percent.

The aggregate participation rate for dove hunting was the same as for duck hunting (1% every survey year). The states that had higher than average participation rates in 2006 were Kansas and Texas. The states with the lowest rate (for states which have estimates) were California, Florida, Illinois and New Mexico.

Figure 41. The State Participation Rates of Dove Hunters Relative to the National Participation Rate: 2006

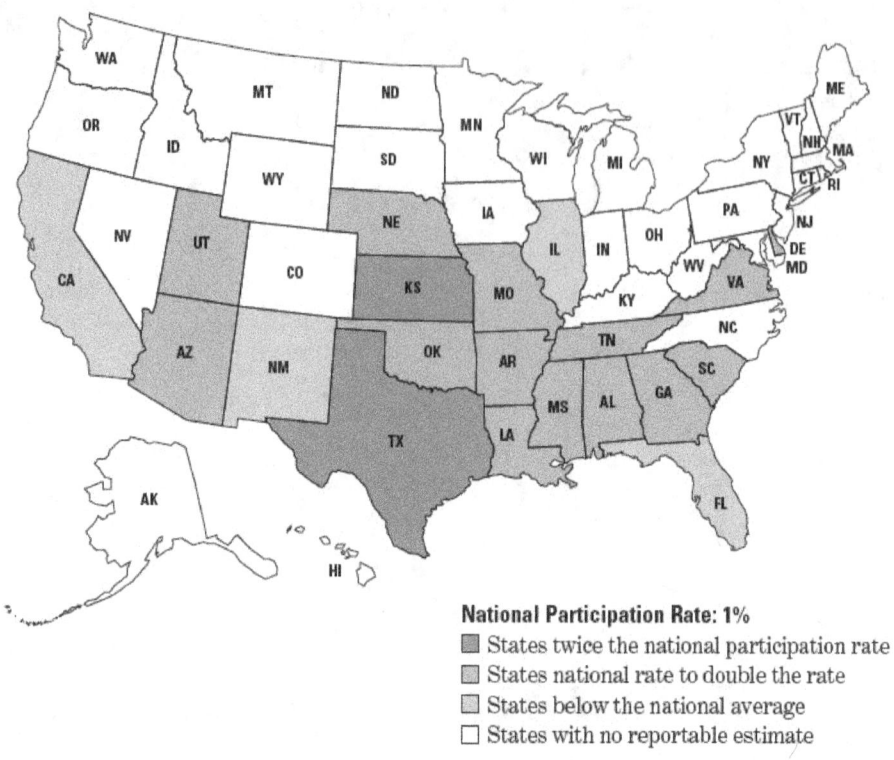

National Participation Rate: 1%
- States twice the national participation rate
- States national rate to double the rate
- States below the national average
- States with no reportable estimate

Table 22. Trend in Number of Dove Hunters, by State of Residence: 1991–2006
(Numbers in thousands)

	Numbers of participants				Participation rates			
	1991	1996	2001	2006	1991	1996	2001	2006
U.S. Total	**1,851**	**1,581**	**1,450**	**1,238**	**1**	**1**	**1**	**1**
Alabama	90	54	67	52	3	2	2	1
Alaska	...	...	...	...	N.A.	N.A.	N.A.	N.A.
Arizona	47	56	35	30	2	2	1	1
Arkansas	38	44	...	24	2	2	...	1
California	183	168	...	109	1	1	...	(Z)
Colorado	29	26	...	...	1	1	...	...
Connecticut	...	...	...	...	N.A.	N.A.	N.A.	N.A.
Delaware	7	8	...	4	1	1	...	1
Florida	64	...	...	39	1	...	...	(Z)
Georgia	63	106	73	80	1	2	1	1
Hawaii	...	...	...	...	N.A.	N.A.	N.A.	N.A.
Idaho	10	...	...	...	1	...	...	...
Illinois	52	57	...	31	1	1	...	(Z)
Indiana	24	...	...	...	1	...	...	...
Iowa	...	...	...	...	N.A.	N.A.	N.A.	N.A.
Kansas	46	38	44	38	2	2	2	2
Kentucky	62	54	45	...	2	2	1	...
Louisiana	73	56	26	42	2	2	1	1
Maine	...	...	...	...	N.A.	N.A.	N.A.	N.A.
Maryland	21	...	...	...	1	...	...	...
Massachusetts	...	...	...	...	N.A.	N.A.	N.A.	N.A.
Michigan	...	...	...	...	N.A.	N.A.	N.A.	N.A.
Minnesota	...	...	...	...	N.A.	N.A.	N.A.	N.A.
Mississippi	50	75	38	24	3	4	2	1
Missouri	54	...	35	45	1	...	1	1
Montana	...	...	...	...	N.A.	N.A.	N.A.	N.A.
Nebraska	27	14	9	17	2	1	1	1
Nevada	13	8	14	...	1	1	1	...
New Hampshire	...	...	...	...	N.A.	N.A.	N.A.	N.A.
New Jersey	...	...	...	...	N.A.	N.A.	N.A.	N.A.
New Mexico	21	16	27	6	2	1	2	(Z)
New York	...	...	...	...	N.A.	N.A.	N.A.	N.A.
North Carolina	91	87	95	...	2	2	2	...
North Dakota	6	...	6	...	1	...	1	...
Ohio	...	...	...	...	N.A.	N.A.	N.A.	N.A.
Oklahoma	58	48	59	37	2	2	2	1
Oregon	...	...	...	...	N.A.	N.A.	N.A.	N.A.
Pennsylvania	73	...	...	...	1	...	...	...
Rhode Island	...	...	...	...	N.A.	N.A.	N.A.	N.A.
South Carolina	55	69	48	25	2	2	2	1
South Dakota	14	13	6	...	3	2	1	...
Tennessee	63	52	65	53	2	1	2	1
Texas	398	279	464	377	3	2	3	2
Utah	12	12	20	13	1	1	1	1
Vermont	...	...	...	...	N.A.	N.A.	N.A.	N.A.
Virginia	66	32	38	39	1	1	1	1
Washington	...	...	...	...	N.A.	N.A.	N.A.	N.A.
West Virginia	...	...	...	...	N.A.	N.A.	N.A.	N.A.
Wisconsin	...	...	...	...	N.A.	N.A.	N.A.	N.A.
Wyoming	...	...	...	...	N.A.	N.A.	N.A.	N.A.

... Sample size too small to report data reliably.
N.A. Not available   (Z) Less than 0.5 percent.

Fishing Participation Rates

There has been a steady decline in the participation rate of bass fishing nationally: 7% in 1991, 6% in 1996, 5% in 2001, and 4% in 2006. In 2006, 25 states had above average participation rates (Alabama, Arkansas, Florida, Georgia, Illinois, Indiana, Iowa, Kansas, Kentucky, Louisiana, Maine, Michigan, Minnesota, Mississippi, Missouri, Nebraska, New Hampshire, North Carolina, Ohio, Oklahoma, South Carolina, Tennessee, Texas, West Virginia and Wisconsin). The states with the highest participation rates were Oklahoma, West Virginia, Alabama, Arkansas, Kansas, Kentucky and Mississippi. The states with the lowest rates were California, North Dakota and Washington.

Figure 42. The State Participation Rates of Black Bass Anglers Relative to the National Participation Rate: 2006

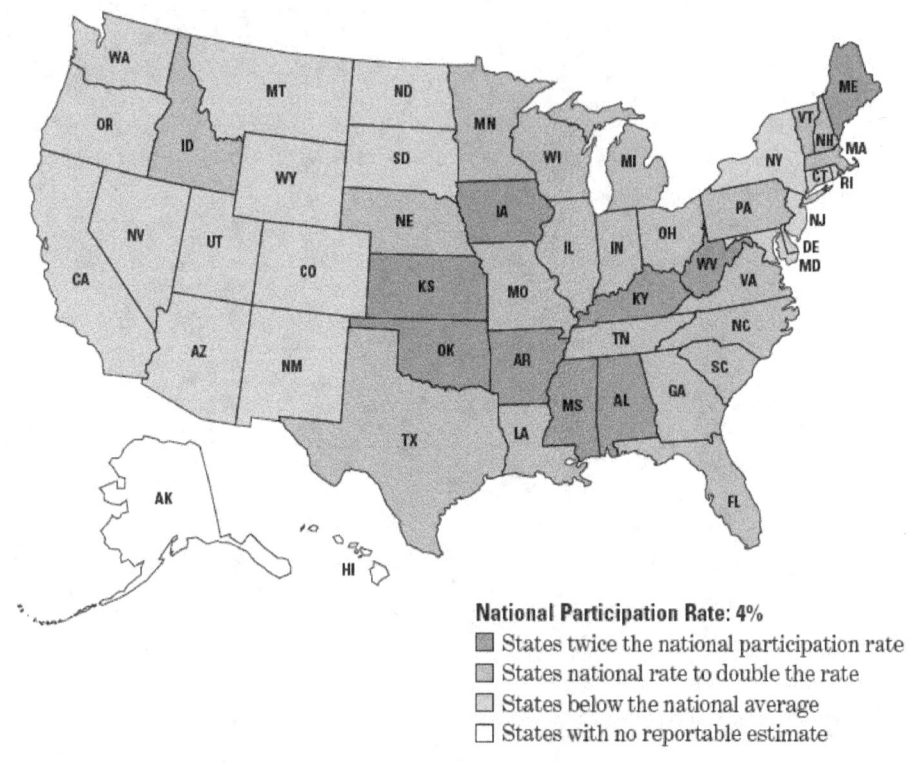

National Participation Rate: 4%
- ▩ States twice the national participation rate
- ▨ States national rate to double the rate
- ▧ States below the national average
- ☐ States with no reportable estimate

Table 23. Trend in Number of Black Bass Anglers, by State of Residence: 1991–2006

(Numbers in thousands)

	Number of participants				Participation rates			
	1991	1996	2001	2006	1991	1996	2001	2006
U.S. Total	**13,139**	**12,972**	**10,956**	**10,181**	**7**	**6**	**5**	**4**
Alabama	340	327	293	325	11	10	9	9
Arizona	145	198	147	129	5	6	4	3
Arkansas	290	201	236	197	16	11	12	9
California	575	691	489	357	3	3	2	1
Colorado	98	102	100	115	4	3	3	3
Connecticut	128	122	101	79	5	5	4	3
Delaware	27	28	18	20	5	5	3	3
Florida	761	626	578	765	7	6	5	5
Georgia	438	454	393	486	9	8	6	7
Hawaii	13	7	...	...	2	1	...	...
Idaho	38	46	38	45	5	5	4	4
Illinois	555	730	508	483	6	8	5	5
Indiana	417	421	360	310	10	9	8	6
Iowa	217	214	185	188	10	10	8	8
Kansas	210	183	175	187	11	10	9	9
Kentucky	336	354	272	308	12	12	9	9
Louisiana	363	351	226	159	11	11	7	5
Maine	67	67	75	83	7	7	7	8
Maryland	213	148	128	130	6	4	3	3
Massachusetts	220	220	162	178	5	5	3	4
Michigan	551	481	310	425	8	7	4	5
Minnesota	245	270	250	276	7	8	7	7
Mississippi	219	213	211	196	11	10	10	9
Missouri	494	515	486	301	13	13	12	7
Montana	11	8	22	21	2	1	3	3
Nebraska	114	90	102	66	9	7	8	5
Nevada	34	41	38	35	4	3	3	2
New Hampshire	80	64	68	56	9	7	7	5
New Jersey	229	253	174	143	4	4	3	2
New Mexico	30	60	37	39	3	5	3	3
New York	557	625	421	315	4	4	3	2
North Carolina	490	437	325	329	10	8	5	5
North Dakota	15	16	10	5	3	3	2	1
Ohio	663	528	562	517	8	6	7	6
Oklahoma	418	310	339	262	17	12	13	10
Oregon	86	74	59	57	4	3	2	2
Pennsylvania	591	506	505	412	6	5	5	4
Rhode Island	37	43	23	22	5	6	3	3
South Carolina	268	335	249	187	10	12	8	6
South Dakota	24	41	18	16	5	8	3	3
Tennessee	382	354	397	288	10	9	9	6
Texas	1093	1231	864	821	9	9	6	5
Utah	16	22	43	46	1	2	3	3
Vermont	30	32	33	22	7	7	7	4
Virginia	372	384	359	226	8	7	7	4
Washington	123	127	107	73	3	3	2	1
West Virginia	143	132	111	145	10	9	8	10
Wisconsin	360	275	339	316	10	7	8	7
Wyoming	6	...	...	9	2	...	...	2

Note: Alaska is not included because its participation rates were based on a sample size less than 10.
... Sample size too small to report data reliably.

There has been a decline in the national participation rate of trout fishing since 1996: 5% in 1991 and 1996, 4% in 2001, and 3% in 2006. Seventeen states had above average participation rates in 2006 (Alaska, Arizona, Colorado, Connecticut, Idaho, Maine, Montana, Nevada, New Hampshire, New Mexico, Oregon, Pennsylvania, Utah, Vermont, Washington, West Virginia, and Wyoming). The states with the highest participation rates were Wyoming, Montana, Idaho, Utah, and Colorado. The states with the lowest rates were Alabama, Florida, Illinois, Indiana, Kansas, Minnesota, New Jersey, Oklahoma, South Carolina and Texas.

Figure 43. The State Participation Rates of Trout Anglers Relative to the National Participation Rate: 2006

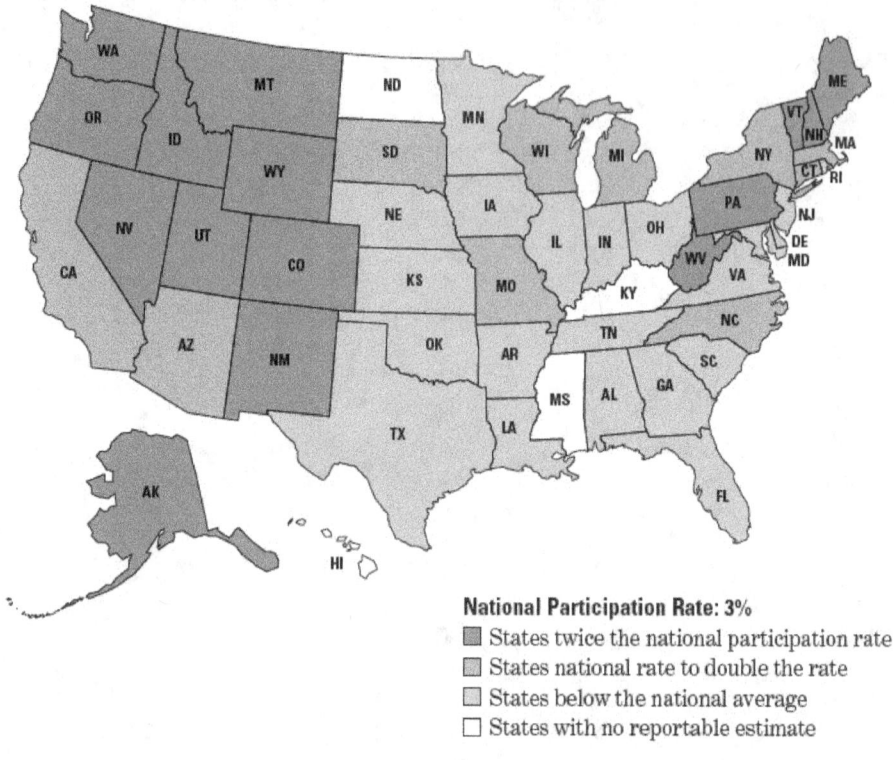

National Participation Rate: 3%

▨ States twice the national participation rate
▨ States national rate to double the rate
▢ States below the national average
☐ States with no reportable estimate

Table 24. Trend in Number of Trout Anglers, by State of Residence: 1991–2006
(Numbers in thousands)

	Number of participants				Participation rates			
	1991	1996	2001	2006	1991	1996	2001	2006
U.S. Total	**9,497**	**9,290**	**8,118**	**7,022**	**5**	**5**	**4**	**3**
Alabama	31	24	21	25	1	1	1	1
Alaska	66	78	67	42	18	18	15	8
Arizona	194	215	214	186	7	7	6	4
Arkansas	66	59	84	41	4	3	4	2
California	1673	1557	1163	866	7	7	4	3
Colorado	490	551	529	478	19	19	16	13
Connecticut	173	170	119	124	7	7	5	5
Delaware	11	14	13	11	2	2	2	2
Florida	76	...	113	83	1	...	1	1
Georgia	120	159	104	136	2	3	2	2
Hawaii	17	10	...	...	2	1	...	...
Idaho	212	252	213	180	28	29	22	16
Illinois	166	235	143	66	2	3	2	1
Indiana	66	44	57	33	2	1	1	1
Iowa	33	57	50	44	2	3	2	2
Kansas	55	41	48	28	3	2	2	1
Kentucky	36	49	41	...	1	2	1	...
Louisiana	51	54	28	62	2	2	1	2
Maine	167	136	124	133	18	14	12	12
Maryland	80	87	112	85	2	2	3	2
Massachusetts	238	218	155	166	5	5	3	3
Michigan	274	248	211	207	4	3	3	3
Minnesota	94	71	62	55	3	2	2	1
Mississippi	18	29	31	...	1	1	1	...
Missouri	181	226	163	146	5	6	4	3
Montana	144	140	174	134	24	21	25	18
Nebraska	43	37	35	29	4	3	3	2
Nevada	108	157	125	128	12	13	9	7
New Hampshire	107	85	82	60	12	10	9	6
New Jersey	248	231	151	88	4	4	2	1
New Mexico	131	165	153	142	12	13	11	9
New York	675	509	384	430	5	4	3	3
North Carolina	163	151	125	202	3	3	2	3
North Dakota	8	8	6	...	2	2	1	...
Ohio	185	121	133	145	2	1	2	2
Oklahoma	60	51	69	26	2	2	3	1
Oregon	346	347	344	306	16	14	13	11
Pennsylvania	809	619	577	566	9	7	6	6
Rhode Island	33	37	22	15	4	5	3	2
South Carolina	40	43	51	29	2	2	2	1
South Dakota	28	38	12	17	5	7	2	3
Tennessee	122	99	121	81	3	2	3	2
Texas	271	253	319	236	2	2	2	1
Utah	216	270	363	266	19	19	23	15
Vermont	68	50	65	41	15	11	14	8
Virginia	174	260	115	107	4	5	2	2
Washington	552	591	462	347	15	14	10	7
West Virginia	113	130	96	147	8	9	7	10
Wisconsin	161	112	158	144	4	3	4	3
Wyoming	101	103	107	88	29	28	28	22

... *Sample size too small to report data reliably.*

As with bass and trout fishing, catfishing has declined in participation: 5% of Americans participated in 1991, 4% in 1996 and 2001, and 3% in 2006. Eighteen states had above average participation rates in 2006 (Alabama, Arkansas, Georgia, Illinois, Indiana, Iowa, Kansas, Kentucky, Louisiana, Mississippi, Missouri, Nebraska, North Carolina, Oklahoma, South Carolina, Tennessee, Texas and West Virginia). The states with the highest participation rates were Arkansas, Kansas, Iowa, Missouri and Oklahoma. The state with the lowest rate (for states which have estimates) was New York.

Figure 44. The State Participation Rates of Catfish Anglers Relative to the National Participation Rate: 2006

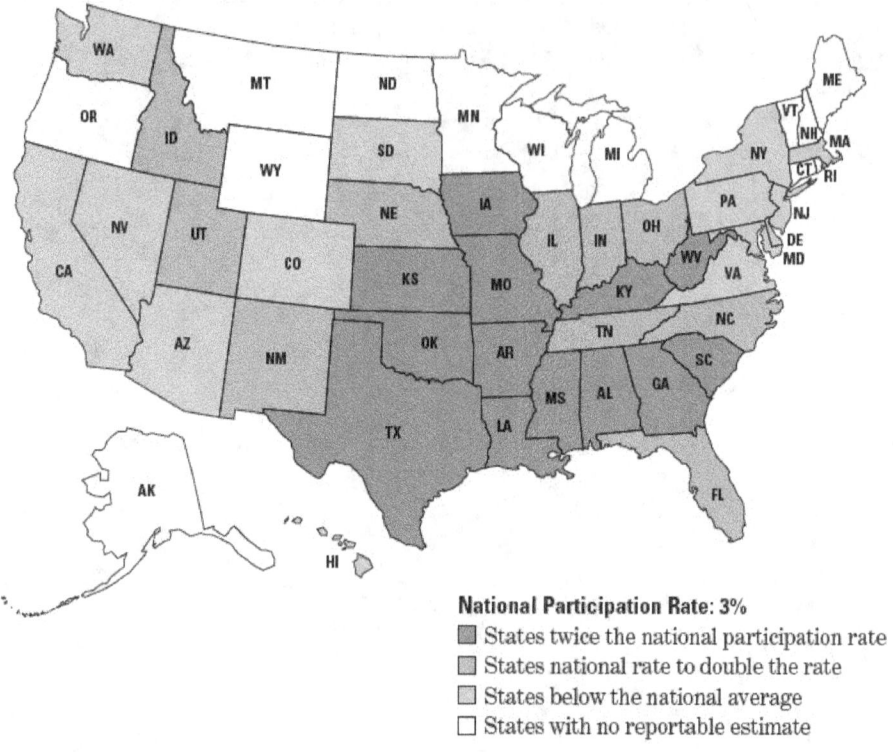

National Participation Rate: 3%
- ☐ States twice the national participation rate
- ☐ States national rate to double the rate
- ☐ States below the national average
- ☐ States with no reportable estimate

Table 25. Trend in Number of Catfish Anglers, by State of Residence: 1991–2006

(Numbers in thousands)

	Number of participants				Participation rates			
	1991	1996	2001	2006	1991	1996	2001	2006
U.S. Total	9,195	7,430	7,517	6,954	5	4	4	3
Alabama	306	284	207	240	10	9	6	7
Arizona	167	110	101	103	6	3	3	2
Arkansas	222	225	271	236	12	12	14	11
California	575	445	403	205	3	2	2	1
Colorado	53	62	79	55	2	2	2	2
Connecticut	34	32	15	...	1	1	1	...
Delaware	15	9	8	7	3	2	1	1
Florida	303	217	280	365	3	2	2	3
Georgia	320	272	456	389	7	5	7	6
Hawaii	10	6	...	6	1	1	...	1
Idaho	25	44	24	31	3	5	2	3
Illinois	619	488	452	353	7	5	5	4
Indiana	325	281	288	211	8	6	6	4
Iowa	289	249	198	214	13	11	9	9
Kansas	218	172	234	205	12	9	12	10
Kentucky	284	248	257	256	10	8	8	8
Louisiana	318	253	195	206	10	8	6	6
Maine	6	...	...	...	1	...	...	...
Maryland	123	74	53	70	3	2	1	2
Massachusetts	52	24	29	33	1	1	1	1
Michigan	130	...	...	...	2	...	...	...
Minnesota	43	...	...	...	1	...	...	...
Mississippi	234	161	229	185	12	8	11	8
Missouri	463	371	429	395	12	9	10	9
Montana	8	...	12	...	1	...	2	...
Nebraska	131	83	91	66	11	7	7	5
Nevada	22	28	30	18	2	2	2	1
New Hampshire	23	9	...	...	3	1	...	...
New Jersey	82	57	28	55	1	1	(Z)	1
New Mexico	40	63	37	43	4	5	3	3
New York	209	129	82	72	2	1	1	(Z)
North Carolina	253	277	274	293	5	5	5	4
North Dakota	7	9	5	...	1	2	1	...
Ohio	424	224	339	284	5	3	4	3
Oklahoma	340	341	308	250	14	14	12	9
Oregon	43	...	47	...	2	...	2	...
Pennsylvania	266	154	164	149	3	2	2	2
Rhode Island	4	3	...	...	1	(Z)	...	...
South Carolina	209	167	231	187	8	6	8	6
South Dakota	30	23	19	11	6	4	3	2
Tennessee	326	230	248	246	9	6	6	5
Texas	1156	1144	972	1001	9	8	6	6
Utah	27	18	31	46	2	1	2	3
Vermont	13	7	10	...	3	2	2	...
Virginia	203	178	171	134	4	3	3	2
Washington	51	...	...	32	1	...	...	1
West Virginia	96	83	84	111	7	6	6	8
Wisconsin	83	...	35	...	2	...	1	...
Wyoming	11	...	8	...	3	...	2	...

Note: Alaska is not included because its participation rates were based on sample sizes less than 10.

... Sample size too small to report data reliably.

(Z) Less than 0.5 percent.

Since 1996 the participation rate for freshwater anything fishing has been flat: 3% in 1991 and 2% in 1996, 2001, and 2006. Sixteen states had above average participation rates in 2006 (Alabama, Arkansas, Georgia, Kentucky, Maine, Minnesota, Mississippi, Missouri, Nebraska, Ohio, Oklahoma, South Carolina, Tennessee, Virginia, West Virginia and Wisconsin). The states with the highest rates were Tennessee, Arkansas, Nebraska, Oklahoma and West Virginia. The state with the lowest rate (for states which have estimates) was California.

Figure 45. The State Participation Rates of Freshwater Anything Anglers Relative to the National Participation Rate: 2006

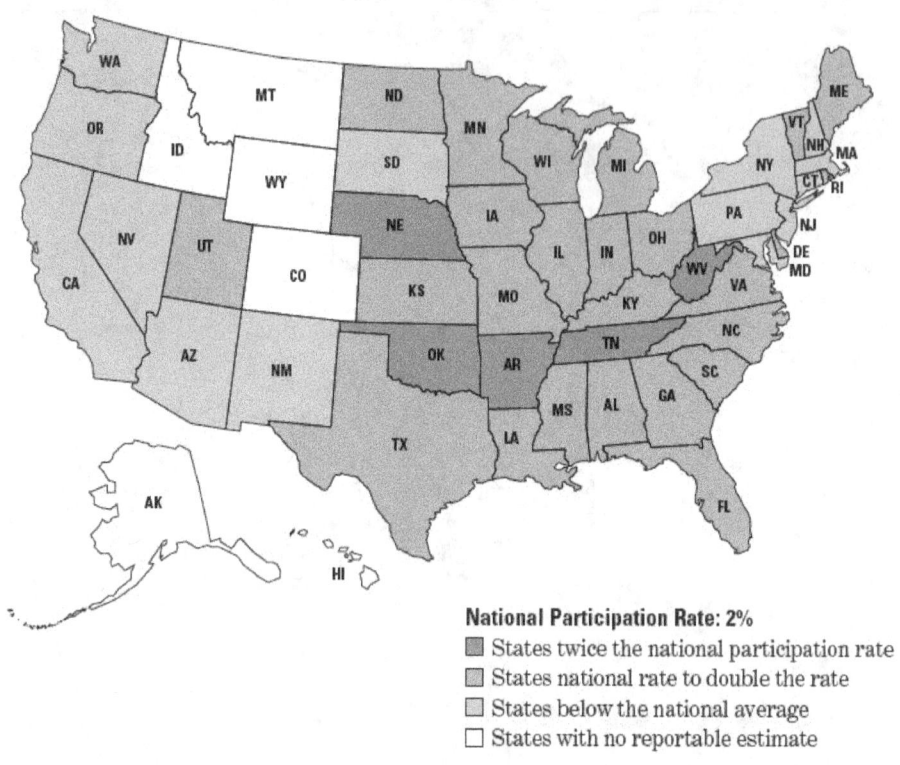

National Participation Rate: 2%
- ▣ States twice the national participation rate
- ▣ States national rate to double the rate
- ▢ States below the national average
- ☐ States with no reportable estimate

Table 26. Trend in Number of Freshwater Anything Anglers, by State of Residence: 1991–2006
(Numbers in thousands)

	Number of participants				Participation rates			
	1991	1996	2001	2006	1991	1996	2001	2006
U.S. Total	**5,285**	**4,475**	**4,872**	**4,120**	**3**	**2**	**2**	**2**
Alabama	90	117	134	122	3	4	4	3
Alaska	3	8	8	...	1	2	2	...
Arizona	49	68	72	51	2	2	2	1
Arkansas	87	70	108	87	5	4	5	4
California	162	243	219	82	1	1	1	(Z)
Colorado	50	47	65	...	2	2	2	...
Connecticut	29	76	55	38	1	3	2	1
Delaware	9	11	12	14	2	2	2	2
Florida	274	212	455	256	3	2	4	2
Georgia	254	136	203	181	5	2	3	3
Hawaii	10	...	6	...	1	...	1	...
Idaho	13	...	...	...	2	...	...	...
Illinois	340	304	267	160	4	3	3	2
Indiana	175	126	103	106	4	3	2	2
Iowa	105	63	93	54	5	3	4	2
Kansas	70	41	62	40	4	2	3	2
Kentucky	136	173	106	107	5	6	3	3
Louisiana	85	128	79	66	3	4	2	2
Maine	30	30	23	31	3	3	2	3
Maryland	60	71	90	59	2	2	2	1
Massachusetts	74	94	100	54	2	2	2	1
Michigan	203	160	132	170	3	2	2	2
Minnesota	113	118	76	129	3	3	2	3
Mississippi	103	49	92	62	5	2	4	3
Missouri	232	96	102	152	6	2	2	3
Montana	12	9	38	...	2	1	5	...
Nebraska	37	23	61	59	3	2	5	4
Nevada	8	18	15	20	1	1	1	1
New Hampshire	14	14	29	14	2	2	3	1
New Jersey	66	53	83	47	1	1	1	1
New Mexico	20	25	19	13	2	2	1	1
New York	339	229	138	125	2	2	1	1
North Carolina	162	149	119	167	3	3	2	2
North Dakota	16	11	23	9	3	2	5	2
Ohio	412	150	212	304	5	2	2	3
Oklahoma	102	142	263	101	4	6	10	4
Oregon	21	...	41	39	1	...	2	1
Pennsylvania	244	288	219	68	3	3	2	1
Rhode Island	12	11	12	13	2	1	2	2
South Carolina	62	95	138	106	2	3	4	3
South Dakota	22	8	17	9	4	1	3	1
Tennessee	159	84	109	215	4	2	3	5
Texas	344	333	267	291	3	2	2	2
Utah	15	...	24	42	1	...	2	2
Vermont	21	14	22	11	5	3	5	2
Virginia	170	111	145	165	4	2	3	3
Washington	57	...	42	30	2	...	1	1
West Virginia	62	46	56	60	4	3	4	4
Wisconsin	150	126	97	135	4	3	2	3
Wyoming	6	7	...	...	2	2	...	...

... *Sample size too small to report data reliably.*
(Z) *Less than 0.5 percent.*

Flatfishing participation nationally has been steady at 1% of Americans since 1991. Seven coastal states had participation rates above the national average in 2006 (Alaska, Connecticut, Delaware, New Jersey, Rhode Island, Texas and Virginia), as well as the noncoastal state Pennsylvania. The states with the highest rates were Alaska, Delaware, New Jersey and Texas. No coastal state which had a reportable estimate had a participation rate below the national average.

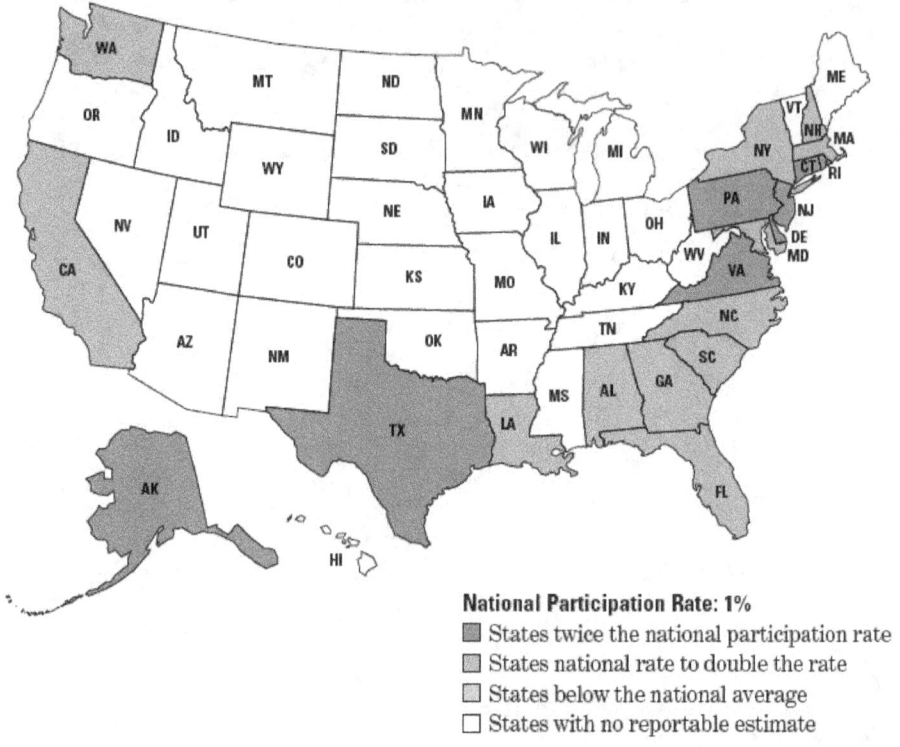

Figure 46. The State Participation Rates of Flatfish Anglers Relative to the National Participation Rate: 2006

National Participation Rate: 1%
- States twice the national participation rate
- States national rate to double the rate
- States below the national average
- States with no reportable estimate

Table 27. Trend in Number of Flatfish Anglers, by State of Residence: 1991–2006

(Numbers in thousands)

	Number of participants				Participation rates			
	1991	1996	2001	2006	1991	1996	2001	2006
U.S. Total	**2,302**	**2,626**	**2,269**	**2,069**	**1**	**1**	**1**	**1**
Alabama	29	25	32	33	1	1	1	1
Alaska	55	67	61	44	15	16	13	9
California	183	211	185	201	1	1	1	1
Connecticut	45	52	51	44	2	2	2	2
Delaware	26	48	28	21	5	9	5	3
Florida	195	233	281	186	2	2	2	1
Georgia	22	55	37	45	(Z)	1	1	1
Louisiana	68	39	48	51	2	1	1	1
Maryland	95	100	60	59	3	3	1	1
Massachusetts	80	62	57	66	2	1	1	1
Mississippi	31	37	21	…	2	2	1	…
New Hampshire	9	7	…	7	1	1	…	1
New Jersey	273	281	180	209	5	5	3	3
New York	220	229	205	92	2	2	1	1
North Carolina	113	205	119	97	2	4	2	1
Oregon	17	…	28	…	1	…	1	…
Pennsylvania	150	188	154	152	2	2	2	2
Rhode Island	15	11	17	18	2	1	2	2
South Carolina	50	75	66	43	2	3	2	1
Texas	321	375	315	447	3	3	2	3
Virginia	118	178	164	97	2	3	3	2
Washington	69	…	35	28	2	…	1	1

Note: States where participation rates were zero or based on a sample size less than 10 are not shown.
(Z) Less than 0.5 percent.
… Sample size too small to report data reliably.

As with flatfishing, saltwater anything has been steady at 1% of Americans since 1991. Ten coastal states had participation rates above the national average in 2006 (Delaware, Florida, Georgia, Hawaii, Louisiana, Maryland, North Carolina, Rhode Island, South Carolina and Virginia). The states with the highest rates were Florida, Hawaii, Delaware and Virginia. The coastal state with the lowest rate (for states which had reportable estimates) was New York.

Figure 47. The State Participation Rates of Saltwater Anything Anglers Relative to the National Participation Rate: 2006

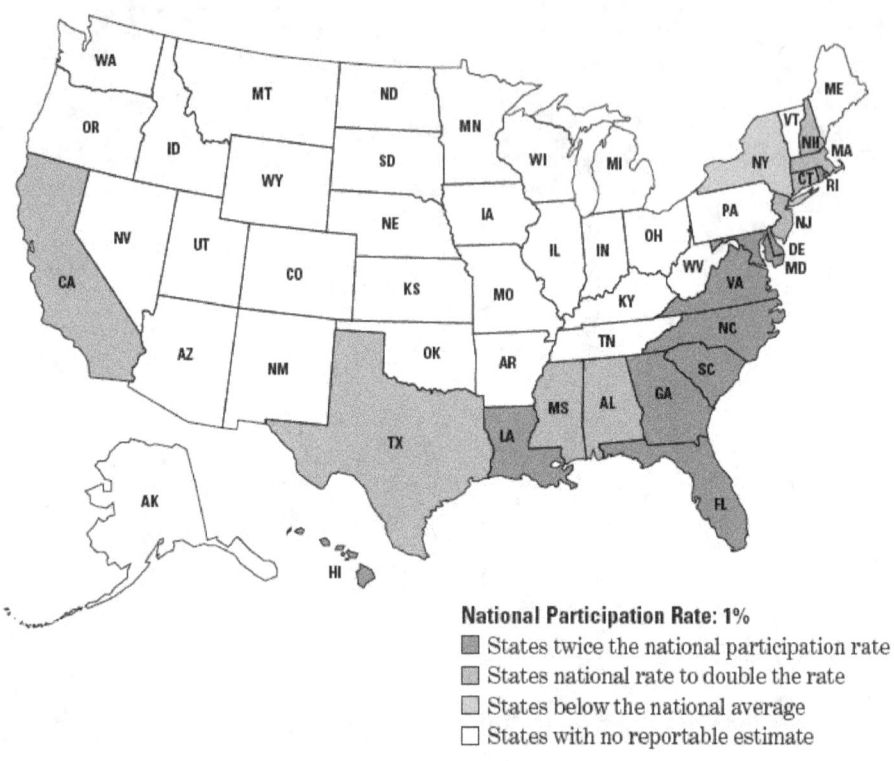

National Participation Rate: 1%

▪ States twice the national participation rate
▪ States national rate to double the rate
▫ States below the national average
☐ States with no reportable estimate

Table 28. Trend in Number of Saltwater Anything Anglers, by State of Residence: 1991–2006
(Numbers in thousands)

	Number of participants				Participation rates			
	1991	1996	2001	2006	1991	1996	2001	2006
U.S. Total	**2,831**	**2,964**	**3,110**	**2,424**	**1**	**1**	**1**	**1**
Alabama	60	47	85	40	2	1	2	1
Alaska	6	6	...	...	2	1	...	...
California	348	284	309	234	2	1	1	1
Connecticut	25	46	51	26	1	2	2	1
Delaware	9	19	15	22	2	3	3	3
Florida	711	743	883	631	7	7	7	4
Georgia	66	104	90	150	1	2	1	2
Hawaii	80	64	64	44	10	7	7	4
Louisiana	71	71	95	63	2	2	3	2
Maine	10	...	...	...	1	...	...	...
Maryland	102	91	127	87	3	2	3	2
Massachusetts	69	77	78	72	1	2	2	1
Mississippi	42	41	49	33	2	2	2	1
New Hampshire	...	11	13	9	...	1	1	1
New Jersey	98	119	111	98	2	2	2	1
New York	98	94	96	58	1	1	1	(Z)
North Carolina	131	198	154	116	3	4	3	2
Ohio	59	55	45	...	1	1	1	...
Oregon	16	...	...	...	1	...	...	...
Pennsylvania	72	85	124	...	1	1	1	...
Rhode Island	13	10	16	16	2	1	2	2
South Carolina	47	71	109	65	2	2	4	2
Texas	296	250	187	210	2	2	1	1
Virginia	140	186	130	162	3	4	2	3
Washington	55	78	28	...	1	2	1	...

Note: States where participation rates were zero or based on a sample size less than 10 are not shown.
(Z) Less than 0.5 percent.
... Sample size too small to report data reliably.

Demographic Trends

Demographic trends analysis gives insight into what is happening to the hunting and angling population. A common use of demographics is to build a profile of the typical angler or hunter. Here, however, we take the opposite approach. Instead of listing the median or mean of each demographic category for a hunter or angler, we find the preferred type of hunting or fishing for selected demographic cohorts. The focus is for which species a demographic cohort is most (or least) likely to hunt or fish.

The proportion of all participants who fall into defined demographic categories is the metric used in this analysis. This enables us to see how substantive the people in each demographic category are in the composition of the total number of participants. Using proportions instead of total numbers of participants facilitates comparison of typical groups of each type of fishing and hunting equally, without having the more populous types be unduly dominant.

Fishing

It is interesting how opposite the preferences of the youngest and oldest anglers are. In 2006 the angler groups that had the highest proportion of 16–24 year old anglers were those who fished for catfish or freshwater anything (the two groups tied); flatfish anglers had the highest proportion of 55 years old and older anglers. Similarly, in 1991 the most popular fish for 16–24 year old anglers was catfish; the most popular fish for anglers 55 and older was saltwater anything. Alternatively, the fish that had the smallest proportion of 16–24 year olds in 2006 was flatfish; the fish with the smallest proportion of 55 years old and older anglers was freshwater anything. In 1991 the least popular fish for 16–24 year old anglers was flatfish; it was bass for anglers 55 and older.

USFWS/Steve Hillebrand

In both 2006 and 1991 the target fish that had the highest proportion of female anglers was freshwater anything, the smallest proportion of female anglers were those seeking bass.

In 2006 the game fish that had the highest proportion of Hispanic participants was flatfish, while in 1991 it was saltwater anything. The lowest proportion of Hispanic anglers in both years were those fishing for bass.

Catfishing had the highest proportion of rural anglers in both 1991 and 2006. The rural population's least popular game fish were flatfish and saltwater anything (tied) in 2006 and saltwater anything in 1991.

In both 2006 and 1991 the angling species that the largest proportion of above median income anglers fished for was flatfish. In both years the largest proportion of below median income anglers was that of catfish anglers.

Table 29. Demographics for Species Anglers: 1991
(Percent of total participants)

	Total	bass	trout	catfish	freshwater anything	flatfish	saltwater anything
Urban/rural*							
Urban	63	60	66	57	62	74	78
Rural	37	40	34	43	38	26	22
Marital							
Married	67	66	67	64	65	68	67
Not married	33	34	33	36	35	32	33
Education							
Less than twelve	16	14	13	22	23	12	14
Twelve	40	41	38	43	37	37	34
College	44	45	49	34	39	51	52
Ethnicity							
Hispanic	3	2	5	4	3	4	6
Not hispanic	97	98	95	96	97	96	94
Race							
White	92	93	94	89	88	95	89
Black	5	5	2	8	9	3	6
All others	3	2	3	3	3	2	5
Household income							
Below median	41	41	39	52	47	30	36
Above median	59	59	61	48	53	70	64
Gender							
Male	72	80	77	74	63	77	69
Female	28	20	23	26	37	23	31
Age cohorts							
16–17	4	4	4	6	6	2	3
18–24	13	15	14	15	13	10	14
25–34	28	28	28	29	29	32	26
35–44	24	25	25	22	23	25	24
45–54	14	13	14	12	14	16	15
55–64	9	8	9	9	8	8	9
65 and older	8	6	7	7	7	7	9

*Metropolitan Statistical Area (MSA) data are not available from the 1991 dataset. Urban/rural designation was supplied by the Bureau of Census, and was based on a modified version of the current MSA categorization.

Table 30. Demographics for Species Anglers: 2006
(Percent of total participants)

	Total	bass	trout	catfish	freshwater anything	flatfish	saltwater anything
MSA designator*							
1 - Inside MSA	73	72	75	65	73	88	88
3 - Outside MSA	27	28	25	35	27	12	12
Marital							
Married	69	70	69	64	67	72	69
No longer married	13	11	13	16	12	11	11
Never married	18	19	18	20	21	18	21
Education							
Less than twelve	13	13	10	19	18	8	12
Twelve	34	35	33	39	33	33	30
College	52	51	56	41	49	59	58
Ethnicity							
Hispanic	5	4	6	6	5	13	10
Not hispanic	95	96	94	94	95	87	90
Race							
White	92	93	95	88	90	89	87
Black	5	4	2	8	7	8	9
All others	3	3	3	3	3	3	5
Household income							
Below median	41	40	38	53	47	29	34
Above median	59	60	62	47	53	71	66
Gender							
Male	75	80	79	73	66	79	74
Female	25	20	21	27	34	21	26
Age cohorts							
16–17	4	4	3	4	5	1	3
18–24	8	9	7	10	9	7	7
25–34	16	16	15	17	20	14	19
35–44	25	24	25	26	25	28	26
45–54	22	22	24	20	21	24	24
55–64	15	16	16	13	12	17	14
65 and older	10	8	10	9	8	10	7

*MSA is the Bureau of the Census' Metropolitan Statistical Area. Very simply, the cutoff for a metropolitan area is 50,000 inhabitants. See the National Survey's national report for further details.

Hunting

In 2006 and 1991 the game animal that had the highest proportion of 16–24 year old hunters was squirrel. In both years the game animal that had the lowest proportion of 16–24 year old hunters was turkey. There was movement in the preferences of the oldest age cohort: in 2006 the game animals with the highest proportion of 55 and older hunters was turkey and dove (a tie), and in 1991 turkey was the game animal (as with fishing, the age groups are opposite-minded in regard to turkey hunting preferences). In 1991 the game animal with the lowest proportion of 55 and older hunters was dove, but in 2006 duck had taken its place. For the oldest hunters (55 years old and older), dove hunting has gone from least likely to undertake in 1991 to a tie for most likely in 2006.

In 2006 and 1991 the game animal that had the highest proportion of female hunters was deer. In 1991 duck hunting had the least proportion of female hunters, but in 2006 rabbit hunting had taken its place.

Hispanic preferences have been quite stable. In both 1991 and 2006 the highest proportion of Hispanic hunters was dove hunters, and the lowest proportion was turkey, squirrel, and duck hunters (a tie).

In 2006 rabbit hunting had the highest proportion of rural hunters; in 1991 it was turkey hunting. For both 1991 and 2006 the game animal with the smallest proportion of rural hunters was duck.

In 1991 and 2006 duck hunting had the highest proportion of above median income hunters. In 1991 and 2006 squirrel hunting had the highest proportion of below median income hunters.

Missouri Department of Conservation

Table 31. Demographics for Species Hunters: 1991
(Percent of total participants)

	Total	deer	turkey	rabbit	squirrel	duck	dove
Urban/rural							
Urban	47	44	40	46	42	56	52
Rural	53	56	60	54	58	44	48
Marital							
Married	69	70	69	62	61	65	65
Not married	31	30	31	38	39	35	35
Education							
Less than twelve	17	17	14	19	23	8	12
Twelve	44	47	47	45	46	36	36
College	39	36	39	35	32	56	53
Ethnicity							
Hispanic	2	2	1	2	1	1	3
Not hispanic	98	98	99	98	99	99	97
Race							
White	97	97	98	95	95	97	97
Black	2	2	2	4	4	1	1
All others	1	1	(Z)	1	1	1	2
Household income							
Below median	43	44	39	45	49	28	33
Above median	57	56	61	55	51	72	67
Gender							
Male	92	92	96	96	96	97	94
Female	8	8	4	4	4	3	6
Age cohorts							
16–17	5	4	3	7	8	4	5
18–24	14	14	14	19	20	17	19
25–34	28	29	28	28	26	29	28
35–44	24	24	26	22	23	25	25
45–54	15	15	15	13	12	13	14
55–64	8	8	9	7	6	7	6
65 and older	6	5	5	4	5	4	4

Table 32. Demographics for Species Hunters: 2006
(Percent of total participants)

	Total	Deer	Turkey	Rabbit	Squirrel	Duck	Dove
MSA designator							
1 - Inside MSA	62	60	60	57	58	70	67
3 - Outside MSA	38	40	40	43	42	30	33
Marital							
Married	72	73	74	69	68	76	70
Not married	28	27	26	31	32	24	30
Education							
Less than twelve	14	15	11	18	16	6	8
Twelve	39	41	39	42	46	30	33
College	47	44	50	40	38	65	58
Ethnicity							
Hispanic	3	3	2	5	2	2	8
Not hispanic	97	97	98	95	98	98	92
Race							
White	96	96	97	94	95	97	98
Black	2	1	1	4	3	1	1
All others	2	2	2	2	3	2	2
Household income							
Below median	41	43	41	50	52	25	34
Above median	59	57	59	50	48	75	66
Gender							
Male	91	91	94	96	95	95	94
Female	9	9	6	4	5	5	6
Age cohorts							
16–17	4	4	2	2	3	3	3
18–24	8	8	8	9	11	8	9
25–34	16	18	16	19	18	20	21
35–44	25	25	24	27	24	30	23
45–54	23	23	25	22	23	19	19
55–64	15	14	16	12	12	13	19
65 and older	9	9	9	8	8	6	6

Crossover Activity of Hunters and Anglers

Deer hunting is the most popular hunting activity for all anglers. Turkey hunting is second for bass and trout anglers; squirrel hunting is second for catfish, freshwater any, and saltwater any anglers; dove hunting is second for flatfish anglers. Duck and dove hunting is last for all anglers except flatfish anglers, whose least popular hunting was for rabbits and squirrels.

Bass fishing is the most popular fishing activity for all hunters. Trout fishing is second for deer and duck hunters; catfishing is second for turkey, rabbit, squirrel, and dove hunters. Saltwater anything fishing is least popular for all hunters.

Table 33. Crossover Participation by Species: 2006
(Numbers in thousands)

Type of angler	Rank of hunting	Number of anglers who hunt for species	Type of hunter	Rank of fishing	Number of hunters who fish for species
Bass	Deer	3,066	Deer	Bass	3,066
	Turkey	1,025		Trout	1,919
	Squirrel	845		Catfish	1,890
	Rabbit	833		Freshwater anything	721
	Dove	544		Flatfish	400
	Duck	473		Saltwater anything	286
Trout	Deer	1,919	Turkey	Bass	1,025
	Turkey	558		Catfish	619
	Rabbit	399		Trout	558
	Squirrel	376		Freshwater anything	183
	Duck	258		Flatfish	115
	Dove	247		Saltwater anything	65
Catfish	Deer	1,890	Rabbit	Bass	833
	Squirrel	655		Catfish	618
	Turkey	619		Trout	399
	Rabbit	618		Freshwater anything	186
	Dove	435		Flatfish	101
	Duck	244		Saltwater anything	65
Freshwater anything	Deer	721	Squirrel	Bass	845
	Squirrel	205		Catfish	655
	Rabbit	186		Trout	376
	Turkey	183		Freshwater anything	205
	Duck	69		Flatfish	90
	Dove	64		Saltwater anything	85
Flatfish	Deer	400	Duck	Bass	473
	Dove	138		Trout	258
	Turkey	115		Catfish	244
	Duck	114		Flatfish	114
	Rabbit	101		Freshwater anything	69
	Squirrel	90		Saltwater anything	51
Saltwater anything	Deer	286	Dove	Bass	544
	Squirrel	85		Catfish	435
	Turkey	65		Trout	247
	Rabbit	65		Flatfish	138
	Dove	57		Freshwater anything	64
	Duck	51		Saltwater anything	57

Conclusion

The generalization that hunting and fishing are declining in popularity is often heard, but is not strictly speaking true. The growth in the fishing population has been higher than the growth in the U.S. population when the base year for comparison is 1955 (see Figure 1). Also, while participation in certain types of hunting and fishing is dropping, other types present a different picture. Participation rates for flatfishing and saltwater anything fishing have held steady since 1991. The same is true for turkey and duck hunting. The number of deer hunters has been remarkably steady since 1991.

The shorter-term trends show a drop-off since the high-water mark of 1991. Since 1991 hunting and fishing participation has dropped significantly. But even in recent years there are areas of stability. Several species hunter/anglers stand out. Turkey hunting is important because it is increasing in popularity at a time when outdoor recreation participation is decreasing. Duck hunting stands out because the demographics of duck hunters are so striking: urban, remarkably high income, and a preponderance of younger participants.

Flatfishing trends and demographics have similarities to those of turkey and duck hunting. Flatfishing participation has not decreased while all other species fishing has gone down, and participants tend to be urban and have remarkably high incomes. Unlike turkey and duck hunters, Hispanics and people 55 years old and older flatfish at a relatively high rate.

USFWS/ Carl Zitsman

Older white males have been the dominant demographic group for fishing and hunting for decades. Youth and women have recently gotten more attention as potential sources of new participants. Squirrel hunting and catfishing have the highest proportions of young adult participants. Deer hunting and freshwater anything fishing have the highest proportions of women participants. Knowing their fishing and hunting preferences could be useful in any efforts to encourage participation.

www.ingramcontent.com/pod-product-compliance
Lightning Source LLC
Chambersburg PA
CBHW052011280526
45793CB00005B/927

* 9 7 8 1 5 0 5 4 6 1 8 6 2 *